EILEEN SOPER'S BOOK OF
BADGERS

EILEEN SOPER'S BOOK OF
BADGERS

**Edited by
Duff Hart-Davis**

INTRODUCTION

by Duff Hart-Davis

NOT UNTIL SHE WAS FORTY-SIX, IN APRIL 1951, did Eileen Soper first set eyes on a badger; but the moment a 'foraging black-and-white snout came into view' as she sat poised above a set in her favourite dell, she was gripped, and she spent much of the next fifteen years studying, drawing and painting her new quarry. Her fascination with badgers became so great that it changed the course of her life, turning her from a professional illustrator of children's books into a wildlife artist and amateur naturalist.

She had always been a country girl, brought up by her father, the artist George Soper, at their home near Welwyn, in what were then the wilds of Hertfordshire. In childhood she often accompanied him on expeditions about the woods and fields as he went in search of the agricultural characters and scenes which he loved to paint; and when she grew up to be an accomplished artist, like him, she frequently sketched landscapes at his side. At home, the family's main delight was the four-acre garden which George created with its fine ferns, bamboos and patches of woodland.

In later life Eileen was always intensely proud of the fact that she had learnt all she knew about art from her father. She used to stress the fact that she never went to art-school, and lost no chance of extolling George Soper's virtues as instructor and mentor. Under his guidance she quickly became proficient at drawing and etching, and in 1921, when still only fifteen, she caused something of a sensation when two of her etchings were accepted for hanging at the Royal Academy, making her the youngest-ever exhibitor in those august halls.

In her teens and twenties she earned a good living from her etchings, and established a considerable reputation in America. Then, when the great depression of the 1930s killed the demand for that medium, she turned to book-illustration, with still greater success. The longest and most profitable association of her professional life began in 1941, when the London publisher Macmillan engaged her to work with that irrepressible spinner of children's yarns, Enid Blyton. For the next quarter of a century Eileen collaborated energetically in bringing to life the Famous Five stories and countless other epics.

She never left home, but lived and worked there all her life. For more than half a century the house was known simply as No 42 Harmer Green Lane, but in later years Eileen called it Wildings. When her father died in 1942, she found herself in charge of the household. Her mother Ada, always a retiring figure, suffered much ill health before her death in 1956, and her younger sister Eva – a proficient potter – was naturally subservient. Eileen thus took the lead in running the house and garden, which gradually became wilder and wilder, until in the end it grew utterly out of control. Its steady deterioration distressed the sisters, but they found compensation in the fact that it became more and more attractive to wildlife.

Both Eileen and Eva were lifelong spinsters: gentle, shy women, devoted to wild creatures, and often enslaved by them. They fed the birds so lavishly that flocks of them invaded the house, pecking the putty from window frames, drilling holes in furniture and book-covers. Being thoroughly soft-hearted, and unable to kill any creature, the Sopers allowed their home to be over-run by mice, which nested everywhere, not least in their slippers and chests of drawers.

And yet, fond though she was of wildlife, Eileen does not seem to have thought of going out into the countryside to look for animals until that crucial year of 1951. Nor is it clear who gave her the idea of studying badgers. No matter: once she had started, she could not stop, and by her own account she put in at least 1,000 hours of observation, most of them at night.

Readers will see for themselves how extraordinarily dedicated she became: out in all weathers, up at all hours, she endured tortures from cold and cramp, midges and mosquitoes, and maintained her vigils even with rats running over her feet. Soon she was not only observing badgers, but also had fallen in love with them, especially with cubs, which she described and depicted with the most disarming combination of realism and affection. I do not think it too much to suggest that for her, childless as she was, these trusting little animals became substitute children. Whenever one came to nuzzle her syrup-soaked fingers, or allowed her to stroke it, she experienced a powerful physical excitement.

Thus smitten, she of course stuck up for badgers, and defended them stoutly against charges of egg-stealing and poultry-killing. She became, in fact, a passionate early advocate of conservation, and her writings form a fascinating period-piece from the days before knowledge of badgers was widespread. She received much help and encouragement from the leading authority Dr. Ernest G. Neal, whose pioneer monograph on badgers had been published in the *New Naturalist* series in 1948. Both in her books, and in later correspondence with individual naturalists and official bodies, she campaigned vigorously against the illegal practice of gassing, which seemed to her as cruel as it was unnecessary, but which was carried on intermittently by farmers. Later, in the 1970s, after she had ceased to write books, she was horrified when the Ministry of Agriculture began gassing badgers on a big scale in attempts to eradicate bovine tuberculosis, which, it was thought, badgers could carry and transmit to cattle.

Her methods of observation were very simple. She would go out dressed in several layers of old clothes – though always with wool on top, so that it would not rustle against twigs – and station herself as close as possible downwind of any set which she thought was inhabited, using natural cover as a hide. From a rudimentary start, her field-craft improved to the point at which she was able to follow badgers about unseen, and remain in very close proximity to them without disturbing their routines. From thousands of quickly-jotted notes, she was able to discern patterns of behaviour which no other naturalist had spotted; she never took photographs, but relied on her sketchbook to capture the sights and events which she witnessed.

This she managed triumphantly. One great joy of her paintings is that in almost all of them something is *happening*. Cubs are rolling, playing, chasing each other, fighting or showing submission. Adults are grooming themselves, cleaning out their sets, suppressing boisterous offspring, or moving gently about the woods. Always there is a sense of family life in progress, as well as a strong feeling for the night. In many pictures a great white moon beams down, reflecting the artist's affinity with darkness. In many ways she herself became a creature of the night, and identified with her nocturnal subjects to an astonishing degree.

For a shy and solitary woman like Eileen, badger-watching was an ideal pastime. Although she sometimes took her sister Eva or a friend along, she mostly went out alone, and she was always extremely secretive about her destination. The dell which she describes so lovingly was in fact less than a mile from her home, but from the mystery with which she surrounded it, it might have been on the other side of England.

The text of this book is taken principally from her first and best work on wildlife, *When Badgers Wake*. This came out in 1955, recorded her observations over the previous four years, and was devoted almost entirely to badgers, with digressions on stoats and dormice. Passages are also included here from three later books – *Wild Encounters* (1957), *Wanderers of the Field* (1959) and *Wild Favours* (1963) – all of which ranged more widely, with a few badger reminiscences among pieces on birds, hedgehogs, foxes and so on. Her final work, *Muntjac* (1969), was devoted entirely to the small Asiatic barking deer which moved into her garden as it gradually turned to jungle.

All these works were profusely illustrated with her own black-and-white drawings; but letters to her publisher show that she would have liked to produce a book with full-colour illustrations. With colour-printing still relatively primitive, the costs proved prohibitive, and the idea was still-born. But by 1956 Eileen had begun to work on watercolours of badgers and other animals, and over the next ten years she toiled as she never had before, completing more than 300 wildlife paintings.

Very few of these were exhibited, or even seen by any outsider, during her lifetime. Every year she sent a few works to the London exhibition staged by the Society of Wildlife Artists, of which she was a founder-member; but, for reasons no longer clear, she secreted most of her watercolours in her studio, and never in her life held a show of her own. Only after her death in 1990 did the true extent of her industry and achievement become apparent.

Other dedicated naturalists have now confirmed many of her theories, and refuted others. But no one has painted badgers with greater feeling or fidelity, and her watercolours will be keenly sought after by succeeding generations.

FOREWORD

THIS BOOK RELATES MY BADGER-WATCHING experiences over a period of years during which I have been able to make notes and keep a pictorial record of the animals, but for those who know nothing of the badger perhaps I should first attempt to summarise his life and habits.

The efforts of a few naturalists have greatly increased our knowledge of the badger in recent years. The difficulties of watching an animal of nocturnal and secretive habits are great. Even now much of the badger's life remains a mystery. How can we tell what happens in the labyrinth of dark tunnels that constitute his home, known to us as the badger's set? We know that he makes only rare appearances by day; that he retires to his set at dawn, and emerges at dusk. Since badgers are very much awake by night, we presume that most of their time underground is spent in sleep. We know that they have large retiring chambers into which they take cartloads of bedding comprising of the most handy material, dry grass, bracken, leaves, herbage of different kinds; anything that is within convenient distance of the set and will make a comfortable bed.

From time to time the sets are cleared, and great quantities of soil and bedding are turned out. Badgers are scrupulously clean in their habits. Bedding is never fouled except by the very young cubs. Then it is frequently renewed by the industrious sow. Soon after the cubs are above ground they learn to use the latrines that are a feature of every badger colony. These consist of a number of small pits dug in the ground some distance from the set. They are used for a given time only, then a fresh area is utilised, and the old one left to sweeten. The badger's set is a model of cleanliness. The fox will leave remnants of fur, bone, and feathers outside his earth to putrefy, but the badger, with very rare exceptions, eats away from home, and keeps his dwelling and its doorstep clean.

What of his life above ground? Ever wary through centuries of persecution, he makes a cautious emergence from his set. Having assured himself that all is well, a hearty scratch is indulged in, though not of necessity, for apart from a few fleas, his regular attention to cleanliness keeps him free from the parasites that plague many other animals. Once above ground he takes his time over his scratching, which he seems to enjoy, but his main concern is to find food. He is omnivorous, and it is not difficult for him to get enough to eat. Even during the hardest spells he can usually find some item of his varied diet.

Having finished his scratch, he will probably wander off on one of the paths leading away from the set, and as we cannot follow him, we must, to a large extent, use our imagination. Careful observation by day will reveal something of his travels. We may find a ditch where he has rooted for grubs; an unearthed mole run where some luckless inhabitant has met a violent death to stay a badger's appetite. A young rabbit's skin, or the spiny jacket of a hedgehog turned inside-out, is all that is left of another victim, for the badger will eat any small rodent to supplement the vegetable matter that forms a part of his diet. His food supply is, of course, variable according to season.

The time of the badger's mating remained a mystery until Ernest Neal established the fact that it took place during July and early August, with a possible extension through September. The cubs are usually born during February and sometimes in March. At birth they are about twelve centimetres long. Their fur, which is then dusky white, shows the facial stripes indefinitely defined, but these are conspicuous in about ten days' time when the eyes are open.

The cubs do not come to the set entrance till they are from six to eight weeks old, and their appearances are then very irregular. Only by careful and patient watching can one hope to see them at this early age. But as they get stronger and more venturesome they become very active, making journeys with their parents and playing together uproariously around the set.

They do not become mature until the spring of their second year, and it is said that the male cubs, at least, leave their parents during October of the first year to take up residence elsewhere; the female cubs often remaining to live in outlying sets apart from the parents, although I believe this to be dependent on circumstances.

At one time badgers were thought to hibernate, but this theory has been disproved by a number of naturalists. There is plenty of evidence that badgers remain active all the year through, though to a lesser degree in the winter months. It is possible that they spend certain periods in hibernation in the colder parts of Europe, but no evidence that they do so in this country.

Our badger, correctly termed *Meles meles* L., is the only species that inhabits these islands. It belongs to the family *Mustelidae*, its characteristic being the possession of musk glands such as those of the weasel, stoat, and skunk. An adult measures from three to four feet from nose to tail, and usually weighs about twenty-seven pounds, though specimens have been taken weighing over forty pounds.

At first the badger appears as a heavy and cumbersome creature, yet he can move with great rapidity if he chooses. His most striking feature is the white head with black facial stripe running through the eyes, and ears which are small and edged with white. The fur over his back is brindled grey to fawn, while his chest and legs are covered with dense, black fur. His tail is about four and a half inches long and is usually pale grey to white. If it were not for these light features he would often pass unnoticed in the shadows. The black-and-white marking on the head is very handsome but is in no way helpful to him. Many a badger might have gone unscathed but for this beautiful but tell-tale coloration.

A further feature is the plantigrade feet; the animal walks on the flat of its feet, whereas in the ungulates, dog, fox, etc, the weight is thrown forward on the toes. The spoors cannot be confused. A clear imprint of the badger's foot will show the broad pad, the five toes, and the claws, which are not retractable, clearly marked. The spoor is distinct from that of any other animal we see in the British countryside.

The legs and feet are very strong, the fore-feet being well adapted to the task of digging the tunnels and big sleeping chambers of the set. We can often see where badgers have cleaned their claws on a tree before retiring at dawn. They have their chosen trees for this purpose. It may be a fallen or a standing tree, and will be used frequently. The colony which I studied first used an old fallen tree that had long since lost all its bark, and the trunk was scoured from end to end with the claw marks of generations of badgers.

They also have their playing trees, easily identifiable by the worn soil at the base, and the shiny bark, for they enjoy climbing on low stubs or trees that have sprawling branches. They are playful animals, and one of the most enjoyable features of watching is to see both cubs and adults at play. A lot of this play takes place when the cubs are present, but hilarious bouts of play occur among the adults, particularly at mating time, when there are wild rushes and stampedes. Then discretion seems thrown to the winds, and the ensuing noise gives away the badgers' presence in a manner that seems incredible in animals of such shy and secretive habits.

The badger is an inoffensive creature. He never picks a quarrel with another animal, and his family life is a very amicable affair. One frequently finds a number of badgers sharing a set on the most friendly terms. They often pay social calls on one another, particularly during the summer months. In fact the badger goes his own peaceful way interfering with no one, which makes his continued persecution by man both puzzling and regrettable. The old practice of badger baiting has long been illegal, but it is doubtful if some of the 'sport' carried on under the name of badger digging is any less despicable.

Owing to persecution the badger remains one of the most timid members of our fauna, and consequently very difficult to observe. He has a keen sense of smell and will detect the scent of anyone who has crossed his path several hours before he emerges. I have had many a promising night's watch spoilt through someone having walked across the set entrances during the day. There is also the menace of those people who cannot resist poking a stick down every hole they see. What they gain by this action I have never been able to find out. Alas for the evening's watch if one of them has been taking a stroll in the area.

Fortunately the vicinity of badgers' sets is often unknown even to those who live not far away. They may be excavated in almost any soil, though sand and chalk are typical. The network of tunnels is usually extensive, sometimes penetrating far into a hillside or comprising a series of 'flats', one above another. They are often on sloping ground, and within easy reach of running water, though I have found sets several miles from a stream, and a considerable distance from even a small pond. Some of the larger sets are centuries old. No one can say just how long badgers have inhabited these islands, but bones have been found with those of the ancient cave bear and other animals long extinct.

The character of the badger has probably altered little, though the fact that badgers are known to have sunning places in areas rarely visited by man suggests that they may have been largely diurnal before the days of man's persecution. Poor Brock gets little peace, yet he is one of the finest and most interesting of our mammals. He is beneficial to agriculture, and his way of life is clean and harmless. In fact he is a grand animal, a valuable part of our country heritage; surely it is time we gave him the protection he deserves.

THE BADGERS' DELL

WHAT IS THE LURE OF THE BADGER THAT IT KEEPS us out late at night in all weathers, cold and cramped, to wait for hours without moving, in the hope that he will emerge and give us a glimpse, or if we are lucky more than a glimpse, of his shadowy form?

I remember well the thrill of seeing my first badger. I had been waiting over an hour in the cold; several times my eyes had been cheated, for the play of wind on the leaves and variations of light and tone can easily be mistaken for a moving animal in the dusk. And when, at last, a foraging black-and-white snout came into view, and a badger made his way towards me through the trees, I stood in breathless excitement, feeling a sense of wonder I had not experienced for years.

Nothing can be as thrilling as a first encounter, yet now that the sight has become almost a commonplace occurrence to me, I never fail to respond with a sense of excitement when one comes into view. It has been said that the badger is no beauty, but to the artist his clean black-and-white head and the subtle curves of his body in movement are an immediate inspiration. And what a striking creature he appears when seen for the first time in the homely setting of the English woods!

It needs great patience and a good knowledge of the animal's habits to see much of him in his natural surroundings. But once we begin watching there is no retreat, for the badger has a fascination few naturalists can resist. The lure takes us out night after night and failures seem only to enhance the desire to try again.

Finding myself compelled to live in a county where badgers were not plentiful, I set to work to make a study of a small and more or less isolated colony. My object was to keep a diary of events and, if possible, to do some sketching of badgers from life in the wild.

I started watching in the dell containing the colony towards the end of April 1951, and on my first watch saw only one badger. But I could tell from what I heard that this was not the only occupant. The extent of the dell was about half an acre. It was sparsely wooded, and outside this area, the badgers had no cover except the hedges that divided the surrounding fields. There were a number of sets in the dell, but it was evident that only one was occupied. No doubt the badgers made use of the others when they changed their quarters, as it is their habit to do from time to time.

Great quantities of sandy soil had been turned out from the main set, which was the one then in use. The sloping side of the dell had become a series of terraces, one outside each of the set entrances. There the badgers would often sit and have their nightly scratch after emerging, or would play for a time before going away in search of food.

Badgers tend to keep to regular paths, and these could be seen everywhere about the dell. A few were obviously used by both animal and man; it was easy to see where man made a diversion around a low branch or bush and badger passed on underneath. Scraps of bedding were trailed along the path leading to the occupied set, and not far from the opening I found two bundles that had been dropped the night before.

The sets were several miles from running water, but a large pond about two hundred yards distant was handy enough for the badgers' needs. A ditch ran down the side of the hedge bordering the pasture to form a small pool at the west end of the dell. At times it brought with it an appalling smell, as I was to learn to my cost on warm summer evenings. A fallen tree spanned the pool, making a bridge for the badgers from the lower bank to the steep one opposite. It was also the tree, already mentioned, where they came to clean their claws.

The dell, which had probably been a marlpit at one time, had a steep chalk cliff about twenty feet deep at one end, and shelved down gradually to become level with the field at its western extremity. Above the deepest part of the dell was a flat spinney of cherry and other trees, with a ground cover of dog's mercury and bluebells. There was also a patch of wild allium; this I noticed was untouched, but there were many places where the badgers had rooted for bluebell bulbs. In the spinney, a few yards from the main set, was a sprawling ash worn smooth with frequent use, for its low branches were well adapted to the badgers' needs as a playing tree. The dell might have been made for badgers. Nowhere among other sets I have visited have I found a situation that lent itself so completely to the needs of a colony.

How often my imagination has been fired by a look round in daylight. Here an old set has been re-worked; there Brock has stretched his full length up a tree, scouring it down with his claws; here are the imprints of his broad feet clearly defined in the soil; big areas of weeds are flattened where cubs have romped together. Plans for watching that night are immediately formed in the mind, and I hurry home full of excited anticipation. Last night may have been blank, but tonight my hopes are sure to be realised. Thus, with the badger-watcher's unquenchable optimism, I set out on my second night of watching in the dell.

I was rewarded with a sight of both the sow and boar and presently I heard cubs squeaking. I saw nothing of them, but I knew it would not be long before they were leaving the set regularly, and there was every hope of seeing them. No doubt I should have some long and fruitless watches, but that did not deter me. The waiting time is never boring to the naturalist, for there is always something new to learn for those who are prepared to watch and wait. There is, too, the enjoyment in the sense of rest in the countryside between the time of dusk and darkness. The sun is going down as the watch begins, and the stars come out slowly, faint points of light between the pattern of darkening leaves and twigs overhead. A late cuckoo calls; the blackbird, always an alarmist, begins his raucous 'tchuch! tchuch!' that advertises his whereabouts to all within hearing, as he seeks out what he evidently fears will be an insecure roosting place. At length he settles down, and all is quiet. A robin, the last bird to go to bed, twitters sleepily; the day closes.

A rustle in the dry leaves tells where a wood-mouse stirs, and presently he can be seen, a little, dark, intrepid figure against the sky, as he climbs the elder bush to melt into the leaves above. Now it is the turn of the owl, the terror of every little creature that moves by night. The eerie hooting begins. A tawny owl is close in the trees overhead; another answers across the field. Yet another, more raucous and imperative than the rest, defies anyone to dislodge him

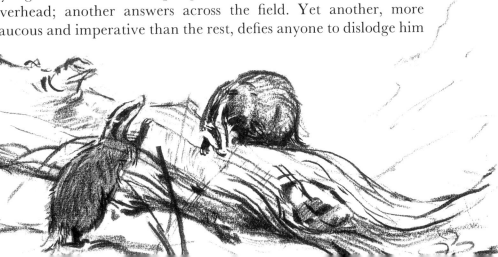

from his perch in the highest tree. But Brock cares for none of these. The ghostly owl is as harmless to him as the pigeons softly cooing, half asleep in the blossoming cherry trees. He has one care only – MAN! He will emerge with every caution and at his leisure.

I never use a hide, but rely on natural cover which I occasionally supplement with a few light branches if I feel it is too scanty. Rabbits come and go, and sit washing themselves or merely browsing, a few feet away, quite oblivious of the human watcher. I often have rats and other small rodents running over my feet at night. On one occasion, after I had been listening for some time to a rustling in the bramble and dry leaves, a mole suddenly emerged, and, coming into the open, shook itself like a wet dog, then passed within inches of my feet to disappear down the grassy bank where I was standing. A short time after, a chattering stoat scrambled over my boots and went leaping into the cornfield beyond. On these occasions I always feel complimented in the way of a bird-watcher who has achieved that happy state when birds pay him no more attention than they do a cow in the field.

I have sometimes felt that a hide would be an advantage when no natural cover was available on the leeward side of a badgers' set, but it has always been my object to avoid drawing attention to the badgers' whereabouts by fixing a hide. The hand of prejudice is too often turned against them, and I have found it necessary to guard the positions of sets with secrecy.

To the experienced watcher hearing becomes almost as important as vision, and we soon learn the significance of the many little sounds of the night. Every rustle seems enlarged in the dark: a beetle stirring from his day's sleep makes an incredibly loud disturbance in the dry leaves, and a hedgehog sounds three or four times his size as he snuffles and grunts his way through the undergrowth. Every little rustle fills the watcher with expectation, and some unfamiliar night sounds can be very eerie and play on the imagination when heard in a lonely outpost long after most of the world has gone to bed. The owls are champions in this respect. For the beginner, nothing conjures up so clear a picture of a tramp lying asleep under the bushes near-by as the 'snoring' barn owl, particularly when his sighs are interspersed with squeaks that render a perfect imitation of a human sleeper in a nightmare!

I must warn the squeamish that a seat on the ground may not be a good choice at night. One evening I took with me a companion who had an aversion to rats. She chose to sit on top of the bank near the badgers' set we were watching. Some elder bushes gave cover and it looked a promising position, but soon after dark two rats ran up the bank chasing one another. Unfortunately, the first sought refuge under her skirt. The resulting chaos put an end to badger-watching for that night. I must admit it needs a stout heart to keep still under those conditions.

The most amusing incident of my early watching occurred when, for the first time, I heard a badger bringing in her bedding. The animal's method of doing this is both wonderful and entertaining to watch. The material used is first gathered into a bundle, which is tucked under the chin and held against the chest. The badger then proceeds backwards, bringing the bundle along with a beautiful arching movement of the head and neck, which is synchronised with the sweeping action of the front legs. Now and then the bundle becomes ragged; it is neatly gathered up again, and off goes the badger once more at a surprisingly fast pace for such an awkward gait. All this makes a lot of noise.

I had been watching badgers for several hours and the night was getting late. They all seemed to have gone away to feed, for there had been a period of silence. I was rudely awakened from my reverie by a loud shuffling noise from the rear. My first thought was that it must be an old countryman returning home from the village pub. His unsteady progress suggested he had been making merry, and was finding it difficult to get along. Presumably he had lost his usual path. He shuffled a little way, then paused as though making an effort to collect himself; shuffled along again; paused once more. I peered into the darkness anxiously, for a meeting with a drunken man in the wilds at that time of night had no great attraction.

Suddenly I saw a badger making her way up the path behind. She was jogging along backwards with a bundle of bedding tucked under her chin, and would pass within a yard of my position. I could only stand frozen in the hope that she would get by without detecting me. But as she drew level she looked up, having noted my scent. She dropped the bundle and raced for the set entrance.

I was distressed to have given her what I thought was a bad scare, and did not expect to see anything more that night. I decided to go, but I had moved only a few steps when I saw her coming away from the set entrance. I remained very still. Unfortunately, my foot was almost touching the discarded bedding. Would she return to fetch it? She came up the path towards me, but when about three feet away, she stopped, then slowly turned round and went back to the set. It was a relief to see her out again after a scare that I had thought might keep her in for most of the night.

CUBS ABOVE GROUND

IN MY FIRST YEAR OF WATCHING IN THE DELL I DID not see the cubs until June 2. I had arrived that night at 9 o'clock and after three-quarters of an hour the boar, sow and four cubs emerged from the main set. I was able to watch them at play and foraging on top of the bank a few yards from me. They climbed on the playing tree for some minutes, then the adults and three cubs hurried down to the foot of the dell making a lot of noise as they went. The fourth cub, finding himself left behind, gave a sudden little skip and hurried after the rest.

The next evening was blank, but on the following night I saw the four cubs emerge with the sow and boar at 9.50. They were delightful to watch as they gambolled outside the set. Several times they came almost to my feet, and they were very noisy and playful. It was a beautiful night, warm and clear, with wood-pigeons cooing in the trees up to 11 o'clock. And when, at last, I was obliged to leave, badgers were all round me in the bushes, playing and rooting for food, apparently unsuspecting. And they were not disturbed as I crept away.

It is always a good time to go when badgers are making a noise themselves. I have often left unheard under such conditions, though they have been very near. If one can emulate the animals' way of walking a few steps, then stopping to listen, they are more likely to be deceived. In this way I have often found it possible to change my watching position without being detected.

Much of the badger's mistrust can be overcome with care and patience, particularly where sets have been left undisturbed for a number of years. As I gained experience in watching I was able to

get better results. My methods improved, and the badgers became more tolerant of my presence. Yet I still had occasional blank nights for no apparent reason.

The most important factor to take into account is wind direction. The wind must be blowing from the set to the watcher, otherwise he will be detected at once. The most vital minutes are those following emergence. Every bush and tree is scrutinised; every scent tested. But once having assured himself that all is well the badger appears to take no further notice of his surroundings, though it needs only a slight indiscretion on the part of the watcher to send him scuttling underground. If he is merely suspicious he may emerge again within a quarter of an hour, but after a bad scare he will not be out for an hour, or perhaps all night.

So far, the badgers had lived in the dell for years unmolested, and though they would, of course, regard my intrusion with great suspicion, it seemed that unless I made any sudden movement or noise I was tolerated. Badgers' reactions to noise are, at times, puzzling. I have known the firing of a gun in the adjacent field, followed by the pitiful cries of an injured rabbit, leave the boar sitting unconcerned outside the set opening. Apparently, the report of the gun and the distress of the dying rabbit conveyed no sense of danger to him. Voices, and people whistling their dogs in the surrounding fields, were regarded as part of the harmless sounds of evening. Yet I have seen Brock jump nearly out of his skin when a rabbit, equally surprised, came on him unexpectedly at close quarters.

There is a good deal of common sense behind the badger's judgement of noise and its danger potential, and in this, distance plays a large part. Even unaccustomed noises fail to perturb if coming from a safe distance. One summer a fair was set up two miles from a set I was watching, and I thought the noise from the loud-speakers would prevent or delay emergence, but the badgers came out at the usual time. They carried on to the strains of a jazz band with a crude nasal accompaniment amplified through the loudest and most offensive machine I have ever heard.

From the beginning of June badgers usually start to emerge earlier owing to the shortness of the nights, and it may be possible to see them in almost full daylight. But any disturbance will delay their coming out, while rain and strong, cold winds will sometimes deter them. My records for 7 May 1951 describe a bitter north wind with a temperature not many

degrees above freezing. The boar emerged at 9.40. He sniffed the ground about the entrance, then returned down the set.

Although I waited for some time he did not emerge again, and I made my way home shivering in spite of a leather coat and other arctic equipment. I was in the same mind as my friend, feeling home was the best place.

The question of what to wear in cold weather is a difficult one. I would not use a leather coat unless driven to it by piercing winds. The same applies to close-textured raincoats, for though they, too, are excellent for keeping out the wind, they rustle and creak against every twig they touch. I have sometimes overcome this trouble by wearing a soft coat over a mac.

The choice of clothes is worth considering. They should be somewhere near the tone of the surroundings; a light-coloured scarf will show up as clearly as a sheet of white paper in the dark, and light gloves will give away every movement of the hands. I have never resorted to blacking my face, though I have sometimes wished I had on a moonlit night when I was certain it showed up like a beacon while a badger stared straight at me. I have occasionally draped myself with foliage in the guise of a paratrooper to good advantage. But this is not to be recommended on a still night when every rustle can be heard in the silence.

Midges are perhaps the badger-watcher's greatest trial in spring and summer. Little can be done to combat the nuisance. And what a plague they were in the dell! The stinking pool also cultivated the fattest and juiciest mosquitoes I have ever met. They were a hungry crowd, too. I have had as many as forty bites in one evening.

When planning to use a new watching position, I try to rake a path to it free from dry leaves and twigs during the early part of the day. This, of course, is not possible in the autumn when leaves are falling all the time, but when it can be done it ensures a quiet entry and exit. To go without being heard is almost as important as getting in quietly: a disturbance is likely to delay emergence for several nights.

Care should be taken not to walk across paths or near the sets before watching. The badger's nose is one of his keenest attributes and he is likely to pick up your scent and turn back from a path you have walked on hours before. Undoubtedly the ideal watching position is found in a tree, but it is not often that nature provides us with such a tree conveniently placed near a set. When one is available it is a great help in preventing the badgers scenting one's presence.

I have watched in many difficult positions, particularly in the dell which is largely composed of steep banks. To stand with your feet at an acute angle can be agony after a while. Similarly I have borne hours of discomfort standing on the roots of a tree overhanging a precipitous bank where the slightest movement rustled a mass of brushwood. But this gave me a chance to get within eight feet of a set entrance, and there I had some splendid close views without being detected.

I was fortunate in my first year of watching in the dell, as the set used by the cubs for most of the spring and summer was the only one that could be watched from level ground. There was a group of hazel and hawthorn bushes about twelve feet from the set opening, and these afforded good cover. A badger path from the set passed within three feet of the watcher, and the cubs and adults used it frequently without suspicion if the wind direction was right.

I used this position often during the first year, but as time went on and I got to know the animals well, I became bolder in my watching, and devised many places that gave me nearer views of the set without disturbance to the badgers.

DAYLIGHT EMERGENCE

A FINE JUNE NIGHT FOLLOWED A PERFECT day, and I had gone to the dell at 9 o'clock hoping to see early emergence. But the sow, boar, and cubs came out late, at 10.20. They gave me a delightful show of play outside the set entrance, then all disappeared down the steep bank. I waited patiently, and it was not long before they came up again on the platform by the set. The cubs were in playful mood; they rolled one another over, biting, snarling, and squeaking with excitement. Presently their gambolling brought them along the top of the bank in my direction. They scampered back and forth, gradually coming nearer, then all at once they discovered a bundle of discarded bedding left on the path. They rolled on it, tossed and turned it, and scattered it in all directions, coming within inches of my feet again and again.

By now the sow had begun to follow, but when she was a short distance away she became suspicious and stopped. She backed a foot or two then paused, gradually retreating towards the set. By her actions she appeared to be trying to induce the cubs to come to her. They took no notice and went on with their play. The sow stood watching from the set entrance, where she was joined by the boar who also stared anxiously at the playing cubs.

Presently one of the cubs looked in my direction. He came forward and stretched out his head till his nose was only an inch or two from my boots. He gazed up at me, a little puzzled but not afraid. I kept still, and after a while he returned to the others on the path. But he was back again almost at once with a second cub. Together they scented me and stared up at my face. Cub number two did not seem very interested, and soon joined the rest. But the first was not satisfied. He went all over my boot with his enquiring little snout. Then he gazed at me again for several seconds, and finally turned away for another romp on the discarded bedding. After a while the cubs returned to the sow and boar at the set entrance. But in a few minutes they were off again, this time to play among the brambles on the other side of the set.

Their sense of fun seemed insatiable. The play went on and on. They were still making a lot of noise when it had become too dark to see them, and I took the opportunity of a rowdy game to cover my exit. It was a delightful experience and one that I shall always remember with the keenest pleasure: this, being my first encounter with any badger which did not immediately regard me as an enemy, had special significance.

The lack of fear was, of course, largely due to the youth of the cubs, and there was no chance of getting on intimate terms with the adults. But there were signs of toleration on their part; examples of mere suspicion when fear might easily have sent them underground at once. There was no doubt that this time and in later instances the sow was aware of my presence near the cubs. On one occasion when two cubs came to the bushes at my feet, the following sow stopped and gazed in my direction. Her actions were interesting. Retreating towards the set, she jerked her head up and back, several times in what might be described as a beckoning motion. After some hesitation the cubs followed her.

The badgers were now coming out earlier, and on June 15 the boar emerged in almost full daylight at 9.20. The sun was scarcely down after a wonderful day. I remember feeling very evident behind my light cover of hazel bush and how impossible it was to defend myself against swarms of mosquitoes.

The next evening was also fine and warm. The boar, sow, and four cubs were out in daylight at 9.15. Every detail of their colour and characteristics could be observed clearly. But even fine nights are no guarantee of early emergence, and it was difficult to explain the reason for a late appearance of the badgers the following evening at 10.30. I had hoped for a repetition of the previous night's daylight performance. When the family did, at last, emerge the sow took the cubs down to the bottom of the dell, while the boar remained at the set entrance. He was furtive, and it seemed something had occurred to make the badgers nervous, and delay their coming out.

A spell of cloudy weather with strong winds followed, and although two days later the badgers emerged at 9.30, they came out with little enthusiasm. They often appear to dislike wind, possibly owing to the noise which seems to suggest an enemy in every bush! Heavy rain, too, is unpopular, and I have seen badgers return at once into the set when a downpour has started just after emergence. A few stalwarts will come trotting out and go away in spite of the rain, but I believe that on the whole they are not fond of wet weather.

During the first year of watching in the dell the steep lie of the land gave me trouble, and many times I was unable to see the badgers when I could hear them playing or foraging down the banks near-by. Apart from the difficulty of finding anywhere that offered cover to the watcher, the banks were very dark owing to a thick growth of elder bushes and foliage of overhanging trees. It was a tantalising situation, but if I had the patience to wait I was often rewarded, for sooner or later the badgers would come my way.

The cubs were very active. They could be heard at the far end of the dell one minute and the next were racing past the watcher, two neck and neck, a third panting up behind in a desperate effort to overtake his competitors. One could not help feeling that a great sense of fun actuated their play.

I tried many different positions in an attempt to watch on the banks. The drawback to any stand down in the dell was the difficulty of getting away without frightening the badgers. Undergrowth presented a problem, and one could not go a foot forward without treading on rotten wood and leaves, or getting entangled in the bushes. One night I stood for hours in a sea of stinging nettles shoulder high, but the rustling made by getting out of them was disastrous.

Yet in spite of difficulties, I did manage to see a lot of the cubs and their play up to July 12; then something happened that put a damper on their activities. For several nights the badgers emerged very late or not at all, and I heard and saw nothing of the cubs. When they did put in an appearance there were only three, and they were very quiet. There was no foraging, and they quickly disappeared in the silence.

During the next three weeks there were never more than three cubs seen at one time, and there was no play. But on August 2, I made a count of four. Much of their old confidence seemed returned, and they were all very playful. Sometimes a cub, showing no fear, would stop and stare at me before going on with its play. Even the adults seemed to have become more or less used to my presence again. On scenting me the sow would sometimes rush for the set, but she was usually out again within a quarter of an hour.

There is no more fascinating sight in nature than a family of cubs at play. They roll and tumble with one another, biting and snarling in mock battle; each very big in his own estimation. The sow looks on and if she is not busy grooming one of the cubs will join in the general romp. All this play is, of course, part of nature's scheme to strength and develop the limbs of young animals. It is a feature of the early life of all mammals, and teaches them to fend for themselves, to catch and devour their prey, and eventually to become equipped for the life ahead. They must learn in the very short time of their immaturity, therefore their urge to play is strong. Watching any young animal, we see that in his play he is perfecting the methods by which he must live. The fox cub pouncing in the grass learns the technique of catching mice and other small rodents. Otter cubs twisting and diving after one another in the water, acquire the agility necessary for catching the elusive water creatures that form a large part of their diet in adult life.

The badger family was now emerging regularly at about 9.15, and would play for long spells on the sandy platform outside the main set when the evenings were fine and warm. It was a relief to have them all together again. I had been troubled by the disappearance of the fourth cub and the general changed demeanour of the rest of the family.

In the autumn the explanation at last came round. One afternoon the farmer's son had been attracted to the foot of a hollow elm by the barking of his dog. The tree was on the edge of the field about two hundred yards from the dell. A badger cub was found crouched inside. It was captured and taken to a farm a few miles away, where it was shut in a strong wooden shed. It was kept for nearly three weeks, and was a great entertainment to the local children. No doubt it was well fed and cared for, but in my opinion the keeping of animals in captivity is never justified, particularly when they are taken from the wild.

By good fortune the shed had a weak spot, the door having been broken at one time and patched with sheet metal. In the end the cub forced the metal aside and escaped. According to my records it reappeared in the dell by August 2. This young badger was never tamed. When approached it would growl and hide under the sacks in the box it was given to sleep in. Its one desire seemed to be to get away from its friendly captors.

The badger has a varied vocabulary, very little of which is heard except by the enthusiastic watcher. Their language, when 'talking' to one another as they sit browsing outside their sets in the starlit peace of a summer evening, consists of a series of low rumbling growls; not very communicative to us, but it has its meaning no doubt. I have often heard, too, the little pig-like grunts of a near-by badger as he searches for food, nose down in the undergrowth or at the foot of a big tree, snuffling into every nook and cranny under the roots. And there are the sounds peculiar to the cubs; the whimpering at the entrance to the set when, impatient to come out, they are held back by the sow who sits resolutely in the opening as she considers the dangers of the night. Perhaps she has heard or scented something that makes her suspicious, or it is too light and she prefers to wait for the protective cloak of darkness before allowing her offspring above ground. And when they do come out, there is no mistaking their high-pitched yelps mingled with very young growls and yaps as they throw themselves wholeheartedly into the enjoyment of their freedom.

Many a passer-by on a lonely road must have wrongly supposed he heard the cry of a moorhen across the fields when badgers are at play, for the sharp, imperative call of the sow can easily be mistaken, by the uninitiated, for the cry of the bird. The sow also uses what I would describe as a low, bubbling call. This seems to be her way of communicating with the cubs, for she frequently uses it when she is with them, and I have heard it only when cubs were present. A variation of this sound, though on a much deeper note, is known as the purring of the boar. It is used to call the sow, and as a preliminary to mating.

Eric Simms has noted a warning call among badgers. He describes this as a series of low guttural 'arks'. It appears to be used as a warning of danger to each other, and is sometimes followed by a frantic rush for the set.

The most arresting cry of the badger is a blood-curdling yell of an eerie quality that sends shivers down the spine of any listener. Mr Simms has made recordings of this during seven months of the year and at varying times, for he has heard it used by badgers within the set, on emergence and retirement, and during other hours of the night. Whether it is given for any particular reason has not yet been established.

DARK NIGHTS

AUGUST OF 1951 HAD A VERY DRY SPELL, AND the badgers were leaving the dell in search of food farther afield. I wondered how they would take to food put out for them. One night, before watching, I put down some apples on the path about twelve feet from the set. Owing to the badgers' keen sense of smell, I did not expect they would touch the fruit that night, although I had taken the precaution of handling it in gloves.

The family emerged at 8.45, and soon one of the cubs came down the path. He ambled along snuffing the ground; suddenly his nose almost touched an apple. He leapt back and sat staring at it. Then, very cautiously, he came to it again and sniffed, his head stretched out, his whole body tensed ready to leap back. He advanced on it in this way several times, swaying from side to side and looking suspiciously at the apple. Finally he overcame his fear and touched it with his nose, but he did not attempt to eat it. He went back towards the set, and after sitting there for a minute or two, made an unexpected rush down the entrance, as though the thought of what he had seen and smelled had suddenly become too much for him. Later he came along the path again and went straight to the apple. Sounds indicated that he was eating it with relish.

Early September brought very dark nights, and I was not able to see much of the badgers, though I heard plenty of activity. Some nights I could scarcely see emergence at a distance of ten or twelve feet. When a badger came close it was only possible to make out a shadowy form. But I could usually hear a lot of scratching, and the cubs were very playful.

A daylight visit showed that the badgers were active in clearing the main set. A great heap of sandy soil had been turned out, and a second entrance, not far below the top one, had been opened. Work was also going on at the two lower openings that probably led to the main set. Two further sets on the opposite bank had been worked, and one at the west end of the dell, previously stopped by rabbit-catchers, had been reopened. Paths were very evident, and the dog's mercury at the bottom of the dell was flattened over a wide area as though the badgers were now making this their playground.

Were the family still living in the main set, or had they moved to another? It was impossible to be certain from which opening they emerged, as light was very poor. On September 6 they certainly came from the direction of the main set; the cubs coming along the top path towards me, with the sow making the low bubbling call I described earlier.

September 28 was a clear, starlit night, but the difficulties of making a count were still great. The heavy foliage of the trees and bushes overhanging the set openings made them very dark. Badgers emerged at 7.40, and by the sounds I concluded they had come from the main set. The cubs were playful, and again I had the tantalising experience of being unable to see them.

Their play reached a climax of excitement by the night of October 1, but observation was difficult. They emerged at 7.45, and went quietly along the path through the brambles. The boar remained sitting at the set entrance. After a short time the cubs returned in a scramble. On reaching the platform in front of the set, one let out a piercing shriek. He sounded badly hurt, and he went on screaming above the general snapping and snarling of the rest. Presumably a not very gentle brother had hold of him by the ear or some other tender spot. The cub was still screaming while they all appeared to tussle outside the set, and finally roll together down the bank. There was silence when they reached the foot of the slope. Only the boar could be heard, still scratching unconcernedly outside the set entrance. Presently the contented bubbling call could be heard coming from the bottom of the dell. Peace reigned once more.

A fortnight followed during which the badgers seemed to have sobered down considerably, and I wondered whether the theory that the cubs leave their parents for good at this time of year was to be borne out in this case. I expected they would leave, as the fact that badgers had been resident in the dell for the last ten years and the population had not increased

(there was only one pair when I began my observations) suggested they had done so in previous years. But on the night of October 12 they were still with the parents.

Clear moonlit nights came in November, and I was able to see the badgers well. I remember, particularly, one on the edge of the field in bright moonlight. He was only a few yards away, and I had no cover. I kept very still, and he sat staring at me for some minutes before making a leisurely retreat to the set.

Through November to the end of January is the period of least activity. Times of emergence are very uncertain, and it is often not possible to watch long enough in the bitter cold one has to endure. Daylight observation shows that the badgers are active to some extent all the year round. Old sets are re-worked, and paths show signs of being in use, for badgers are out on most nights, even when the ground is snow covered.

It is known that they can go without food for long periods, but they go out to glean what they can almost nightly, and often travel long distances in their search. One path used by the dell badgers crossed several fields and a deep lane to reach woods on the horizon. I knew it was used through most of the year, and when the snow came I was able to track it a long way, but eventually lost the spoors in a snow-drift. I found only one place under a hedge where Brock had scratched out some morsel of food, and unless he fared better farther on he must have had a lean night.

PERSECUTION

TWO OPENINGS IN THE SAND BANK, BELOW THE main set, had been in use during the winter, and the main set was cleared out by the end of February. I began to think there might be some hope of cubs having been born there. Bedding and a large amount of sand were turned out, and paths leading from the set were obviously in frequent use. Sand carried in the badgers' fur could be seen scattered along them for a considerable distance. By the second week in March there was still no reliable evidence that cubs had been born. There was not much sign of activity. Moonlight gave little reward, and the dell was often silent long after badgers should have emerged.

About this time, I heard of a colony nearer home and went, at once, to investigate. I was delighted to find several sets where badgers were in residence. They were on the slopes of a wood some distance from habitation, and I had hopes for survival as the land was not reserved for game. Where a keeper knows his job, all is well, but where he is ignorant of the badgers' true habits, they, with many more innocent members of British wild life, are destroyed in the mistaken belief that their existence is harmful to game preservation.

I made plans to divide my watching between the newly found sets and those in the dell. The wood was situated above a valley used by the army during the war. Old dugouts, huts, and latrines, falling into decay, littered the valley. Firing slits and broken windows seemed to have eyes as one crept past them in the dark. And to add to the hazards, there was always the chance of coming face to face with a huge Friesian bull that sometimes broke loose

from the pasture, and might be found wandering anywhere.

The wood was extensive, and apart from some timber felling and carting in the previous autumn, it had remained practically unmolested for years. The way out, unless one crossed the badgers' sets, had to be along the ridges where the timber waggons had cut deeply into the mud. The ruts were waterlogged, and it was no mean feat to walk on the high slippery ridges in the dark, particularly on legs that had become unsteady through hours of standing.

The weather turned very cold towards the end of March. Snow came by April 1, and I went to the wood in daylight. The sun was out, and the snow had already started to drip from the trees, but I was able to see where a badger had emerged the night before. I followed his meandering path for a long way, as I hoped to find out his destination, but his wanderings through the tangled undergrowth were so involved that I had to give up.

The spring was before us, and I had every hope that this would be a rewarding colony. But before I could do any further watching there, the badgers were all killed.

Visiting the wood one clear spring morning, I found every set stopped. Gas had been used, and there was no sign that any badgers had lived to make their way out. To complete the scene of destruction, motor-cyclist rough-riders had held tests over the sets, cutting up the ground till the wood was a quagmire.

It was one of the rare mornings that seem to give us nature's reward for winter; when everything that has struggled through the lean, hard days now finds fulfilment in the joy of living and feeling the warmth of sunlight again; when the whole countryside teems with life and industry. My thoughts turned to the badgers lying dead beside their cubs. It is not surprising that animals go in fear when they can die choked by something unseen and unheard in the den that was their only hope of security.

There is no excuse for killing a badger at any time unless he has turned 'rogue' and through unnatural circumstances deviated from his usual diet and taken to killing poultry. But the 'rogue' badger is a rare occurrence. To destroy a whole colony of beneficial animals by gassing because one has turned 'rogue' is both cruel and illogical.

It is only through sheer tenacity that the badger has managed to survive in Britain at all. Various crimes are unjustly laid at his door, and he continues to be persecuted by many who should know better. Much of his normal food consists of pests harmful to agriculture. He does excellent work in clearing the land of grubs that would destroy crops, and contributes largely in keeping down the rabbit population by digging out nests of young rabbits. Rats, mice, moles, and other small rodents are taken with relish, and there is nothing he likes better than to root out a nest of wasp grubs. In badger country one can often see where they have been at work, and I have known them to travel several miles night after night clearing the land of a plague of wasps' nests.

A great deal of reliable evidence has been collected by naturalists who have made a scientific study of the habits and food of the badger, and it has been established, and acknowledged by agricultural authorities, that he is beneficial to the land in general. It is advised that he should be allowed to remain unmolested. Yet prejudice and ignorance of his ways still exist and produce a state of mind in many landowners that is closed to all reasonable argument. If it is known that a badger is in the district, every loss of poultry, game, and even lambs is attributed to it.

No one has ever produced conclusive evidence of a lamb being killed by a badger. Remains of dead lambs are said to have been found outside badgers' sets, but this is no proof of guilt. Badgers very rarely take food back to their sets, but foxes frequently do, and as it is not unusual for a fox to take up residence near, or even in, a badger's set, the badger is blamed for the fox's misdeeds.

It is sometimes alleged that badgers take game birds' eggs, but there is no reliable evidence that they are guilty on that score. It may happen once in a while, but pheasants have been reared successfully within a few yards of badgers' sets.

As for poultry killing, hundreds of cases attributed to badgers have been proved, with very rare exceptions, to be the work of foxes. Howard Lancum has done valuable research on this. His figures are convincing: out of 109 cases he investigated he proved 92 to be due to foxes with a loss of 552 birds; in 15 cases the culprits could not be identified, while only two cases were proved against the badger, and these with a loss of no more than two birds.

Turkeys were reared on a farm near badger sets I was habitually watching. The young birds were herded together in small wire enclosures and wooden houses that a badger could easily have broken into. They were not more than a hundred yards from the sets, and I knew badgers must pass near as there was ample evidence of their rooting for grubs in the big, rotted manure heap just beyond. The turkeys were never touched.

As another instance, I went to investigate a report that some poultry had been killed by a badger on a farm three miles from my colony. The farmer had an interesting story. He had lost four chickens at night, and when, next day about 1 o'clock, he saw a badger by the farm pond, he immediately came to the conclusion that it had taken the poultry. The badger was too far off to be shot with certainty. The farmer fired twice and missed.

"I'm thankful I did," he said as he went on with his story. The next night he lost four more chickens. Snow was on the ground, and fox's footprints showed up clearly round the poultry houses.

That week an article appeared in a well-known farming journal giving the true facts about badgers. It spoke highly of their value to agriculture. The farmer read it. He was delighted to think that he might have a badger in residence on his land, and asked me to go to a small chalk pit and identify what might be a badger's set. He had been ready to gas the holes there, but after the incident, had stayed his hand.

I found badger spoors; paths that were obviously used by a badger, and other signs that one was in residence. It was disappointing when the badger left during the summer of that year. It seemed he was a bird of passage, unless he had fallen a victim to someone less enlightened than my farmer friend.

BADGERS AND NIGHT BIRDS

I CONTINUED TO WATCH FREQUENTLY IN THE DELL, but the badgers seemed very quiet and inactive. The weather was not encouraging, and long, cold waits often went unrewarded or gave no more than a glimpse of a black-and-white head in the set opening. Yet by daylight sets were seen to have been turned out with great vigour. This was evidently being done late in the night, and even my enthusiasm could not combat the rigours of waiting more than three hours for emergence in the exceptionally cold weather we were having.

By the second week in April the nights became warmer. Things livened up a little, and I saw three and possibly four badgers out on the night of April 13. There was some play and a lot of scratching; the badgers often remaining for long periods by the sets. How Brock enjoys a scratch! His long claws are well adapted for the purpose, and I believe that much of this scratching is a means of grooming the coat. Badgers are not verminous, and it seems unlikely that the scratching is caused by the few fleas they may have; most of it appears to be indulged in out of sheer enjoyment.

It is said that the sow has cubs every year, and towards the end of April I intensified my watching in the hope of seeing cubs above ground at an early age. Work was being done on the main set and on the set at the north-east corner where a lot of bedding was turned out with the soil. This raised my hopes of cubs having been born there, but difficulties of watching this set were great. It was at the steep end of the dell, and the only positions were on the edge of the field to either side of the set.

The watcher had to stand with a steep cliff in front and a cow of very uncertain temperament in the field behind! No one but the cowman could handle her, and if she happened to see anyone enter the field, she would immediately come after the intruder, who was wise to make a hasty retreat. Needless to say, I always tried to keep an eye on her, which was not easy in the dark. Watching here was a little strained. The only way of escape, should she decide to be difficult, was a sheer drop into the dell.

If the difficult cow was not in the field, a herd of forty Friesians took her place, and would usually choose this end of the dell for the first hours of the night. They stamped, rubbed against the trees, caught their horns in the boughs, snorted, coughed, and made themselves a general nuisance. I always hoped the bull, who shared the field with them by day, had not been left out! I do not think the noise from the cows would have worried the badgers, as the field had been used for pasture for as long, or longer than the colony had been there, but, for some reason, I had little result at this set, and after a while I transferred my attentions to the old and main set.

The wind forced me to wait to the east of the entrance, and I had to stand on a narrow board spanning the top of the slope and a tree where the slightest movement rustled a mass of brushwood. Later I improved the situation considerably, and it became my chief watching position when the wind was in the west, but at that time the discomfort there was almost intolerable. On the night of May 5 I endured three and a quarter hours, hoping to make a count and find out whether last year's cubs were still with the parents. I saw only one badger emerge.

It was a disappointing evening, but the nightingales were a great compensation. It was midnight when I reached the common, where the yellow flowers of the gorse were lit by a brilliant full moon. A nightingale was singing close beside me in a thicket, another but a few yards away and yet another in the hedge beyond. As I listened, I heard the songs of others farther and still farther afield, and it seemed that the singing must go on for miles throughout the countryside, to imbue the still air with a sense of fantasy that took the listener into a world apart from everyday life where our encounters are too brief.

Only those who take the trouble to stand out in the woods or fields can have any idea of the number of voices to be heard after dark. Some are more weird than beautiful, others in their perfection seem as mysterious as the starlit sky. Among these are the songs of several of the warblers, but we must give pride of place to the nightingale. To stand under a full moon on a warm May night listening to this bird is a moment in life that can have few equals.

Could we see into the night we should, no doubt, be surprised at the number of birds on the wing after dark, particularly in times of migration. Birds not normally seen or heard in one's own district can be identified by their unfamiliar calls as they pass on long journeys. Watching in the badger dell I have often noted the soft hush of flocks of passing migrants, and I have heard the cry of whimbrel and the drumming of snipe among the night fliers. Snipe frequent my home district, but these were passing migrants, staying only a week in the vicinity of the dell, on their way to some marshy and, to them, more desirable corner of Britain.

But apart from the owls, the peewit was the most frequent voice of the spring nights. At this time of year the cock bird seems tireless, for he is on the wing most of the day and continues his flight till long after midnight. The beautiful wailing call accompanies what might be described as an aerial dance as he sweeps and tumbles in rapturous flight, often beneath a moonlit sky that sets the stage for one of the most beautiful courtship displays of the spring. His movements are difficult to follow, even with the guiding cry and the loud rhythmic creak of the wings, for one moment he sweeps low over the field, and the next is up and away into the sky with a glorious abandon from which he as rapidly tumbles loose-limbed to earth, recovering when only a foot or two from the ground to wheel up again, no more than a ghostly voice of the sky.

Usually the spring or summer night will break into life with the coming of dusk, and teem with the industry of bird and beast. Yet there are nights full of promise that remain strangely silent: still windless nights with clear skies and warm summer air that seem to offer everything desirable to the creatures of the wild. Yet no badger stirs. Hours go by and and the fields and hedges seem deserted. We miss the peewit's plaintive call; the owls are silent; no mouse rustles the undergrowth, and the watcher might be the only living creature abroad. Such nights occur in every watcher's diary, and they are unaccountable. No doubt there is some cause for these silent nights, some reason for the inactivity of all wild life. It is a mystery that we are never likely to solve.

SUMMER WATCHING

THE BADGERS WERE NOT EMERGING TILL 10 P.M. which gave little opportunity to make a count in the poor light. But they came out regularly, and bedding was brought on several occasions. Daylight visits showed this to be comprised of bluebell flowers and foliage. A bundle was left at the set entrance. This unwittingly delightful habit of lining the bed with flowers is not confined to badgers. I once saw a very beautiful moorhen's nest on the edge of a small pond in a field; the eggs were lying in a cradle of buttercups.

For some time emergence had been from the lower set opening, but on May 20 the badgers came from the top entrance, and I was able to get a better view. Only two were seen to emerge, but others were heard down the bank. Noise of great activity came from the bottom of the dell, and once there was a wild scamper that brought several badgers up round the main set opening.

Next morning I was able to see where the ground was beaten flat in the shape of a figure eight around the elder bushes in the foot of the dell. I was still anxiously looking for signs that this year's cubs, if any had been born, were above ground. A lot of bedding and soil had been turned out from the corner set at the steep end of the dell, but this proved nothing as badgers often clean out sets they are not using at the time.

Towards the end of May bedding was frequently brought to the main set, and a number of other sets were spring cleaned. On May 27 I saw two of last year's cubs emerge with the boar from the main set, and during the following week, when there was a lot of activity, they often took part in the work of collecting bedding.

The industry of these bedding collections was great. On the night of June 9, bundles were brought at ten-minute intervals for a long time, and June 15 was a particularly busy night. Waiting six feet from the set entrance, I watched two badgers make their way up the bank from the lower opening. I was not seen, and after an inspection of the main entrance, they went away along the path.

Presently the sow came back with bedding which she took into the main set. In a minute or two she was out again, scuttling away in a hurry to get some more. Before she could return, the boar came in with his bundle, and he, too, went out quickly for the next lot. They kept this up till they had brought in sixteen bundles, the last being taken to the lower set opening. Though the cubs came out, they took no part in the work that night.

The badgers' habits were different from last year. There was no play; no sitting outside the sets for a nightly scratch. Where did they go? What did they do when they wandered away into the shadows where I could not follow? They were evidently not feeding in the dell as they had at the same time last year when the cubs were young.

Parents and three cubs were now living together, and it was certain no cubs had been born that spring. What had happened to the fourth of last year's cubs? Had he been the wanderer fortunately missed by the farmer's gun?

At this time we had a spell of bad weather with rain and wind in plenty. I continued to watch, but not a badger did I see for several nights. But when June 23 gave a fine, clear evening, the boar emerged from the main set at 9.45. I saw no further activity till 10.30 when the sow and one of last year's cubs came from the lower opening and went away through the bushes.

Very soon I heard the sow returning with bedding which she took into the main set. A big collection began. Backwards and forwards they went with their bundles, all five badgers taking part. There seemed to be a great urgency about the work. They came one after another, shuffling along with the bedding, to go down into the set, and come out again in no time. Away they ran, passing close to where I stood in the hazel bush, and on, unsuspecting, down the path near my companion.

The coming and going was continuous for so long that I lost count of the number of times bedding was brought. Apparently, all this cleaning and renewal of bedding was a preliminary to leaving the set, as several nights after this they vacated it, and went to another.

Fine weather followed. Larks sang up to 10 p.m. on the rare starlit evenings, and we had the warmest June night for five years. That evening I expected to see the badgers out before dark, but it was not till 10.30 that I heard one scratching on the bank below me. There was some play at the bottom of the dell, and I stayed till a late hour but saw very little. Light now seemed to have no bearing on times of emergence, and it was not possible to account for a number of late emergences on those perfect nights.

On July 19 the badgers were back in the main set. By the time they came out it was too dark to make a certain count, but several of them emerged in spite of a lot of noise from a fair not far away. The chalk set, west, had been worked again, and a new hole opened on the edge of the cornfield. An area of grass was flattened beside it, and paths led into the corn, which suggested that at least some of the badgers were in residence there.

I changed my vantage-point to one overlooking the cornfield. After emergence the badgers went into the corn, and I listened to the continual rustling as they meandered back and forth. I examined the field by daylight, and found that only an occasional ear of wheat had been taken. No doubt rats and mice were the attraction, with the lesser fry of various grubs making a helpful addition.

I noticed that the cubs, now in their second year, were still less aware of danger than the parents, and therefore easier to watch. They would come very close and would sometimes follow the track of one's footsteps, nose down, showing no reaction, whereas the adults would have at once scented danger, and fled.

The foraging in the wheatfield ceased with the coming of bad weather, and the corn was cut on August 12. A lot of work was now being done at the three openings to the main set, also at the chalk set, west. The new entrance on the edge of the field had been deserted when the corn was harvested. Many sets were being worked, and it became almost impossible to tell which were occupied. If I waited at the chalk set the badgers came along the path from the main set; if I waited at the main set I heard them emerging from the opposite bank. It seemed they were always changing house, and I was never in the right place.

It was near the end of September, and the weather was poor with cloudy skies and strong wind. When at last we did get a promising night, it was upset by a poaching gipsy who scurried furtively into the dell as I and a companion arrived. We ignored him, and took up positions to watch the set at the west end of the dell, but near the time of emergence he appeared again. We saw him creeping along the edge of the dell behind us, and presently he fired at a rabbit near-by. This put an end to the proceedings as far as watching was concerned.

Three of the previous year's cubs were still with the parents at the beginning of October, and one night I saw four out of the five badgers come from the lower set opening and make for the level ground at the top of the dell under a big oak. An acorn feast quickly developed.

Badgers are noisy feeders, and it was amusing to hear the acorns relished. They were first turned round several times in the mouth with loud guzzling sounds of approval, then cracked under the teeth, and chewed and champed with much smacking of chops.

About half a minute was given to each acorn before it was swallowed, then another was immediately sought.

Soon all the badgers were at the feast, and the acorns that were easily found had been eaten. A further search started among the leaves and brambles. The food was taken with a gourmet's relish. Nobody was handicapped by manners, and it was every man for himself, with scratching a feature of the party.

The next night an attempt on my part to watch from a closer position made the first badger suspicious, and I had the tantalising experience of hearing a feast going on under another oak in the bottom of the dell. From August 25 many sets were being cleared out, and this work reached its height during September and October when great quantities of soil and discarded bedding were turned out of a number of sets. This preparation for winter is general in badger communities. Sets are occupied for a limited time, then cleaned and left to freshen while others are used. The animals take the opportunity to line their sleeping quarters with plenty of dry bedding before the worst of the weather sets in. They will occasionally gather bedding when the grass is wet, but it is usual to collect dry material.

The badgers had now reached their quietest season, and I planned to see all I could of their activities during the coming winter, but fate, as the next chapters will show, intervened to upset my plans and those of my quarry.

FINDINGS FOR THE YEAR 1952

The conclusions drawn from the year's watching showed that badgers do not necessarily breed every year; that times of emergence had been, in general, later than throughout last year when cubs were born, and there was also a marked difference in behaviour. They were less active and the demeanour of all had been considerably quieter.

THE GASSING

BLACK CATS ARE SAID TO BRING GOOD LUCK, but perhaps their luck dies with them. It certainly died with the one I found shot at the bottom of the dell in December. From then on, a spell of bad luck started for the badgers.

On January 6 I saw that the set entrances had been much trampled, presumably by those who had pushed the dead cat down one of the holts. But there was evidence of plenty of activity by the badgers. Paths were well worn, and they had been digging for bluebell bulbs in the spinney. A fortnight later, most of the elder bushes were cut down at the bottom of the dell, and the sets were again disturbed; many foot-marks trampled the entrances.

Illness intervened, and I was unable to get to the dell till March 14. It was distressing to find all the sets stopped. Soil had been packed into the entrances following the use of gas. I could find no sign that any badgers had escaped; there was no evidence of activity.

Two days later I visited the sets again, and, to my delight, found that badgers were active. Some had evidently lived to get out, but had been lying up quietly till they thought the danger past.

I now discovered that they had sought refuge in a set that they had opened at the steep end of the dell. It was situated under the roots of an ash tree that clung precipitously to the chalk cliff. The opening to the set was about six feet down from the top of the cliff which was almost perpendicular. A foot below the set entrance there was an undercut and a sheer drop of about eight feet to the slopes below. Soil had been turned out there, and several big bundles of unused bedding had fallen from the cliff.

After a day or two I found sand scattered by the badgers along the paths near the main set. They had also been active on the sandy platforms, and were evidently showing interest in the sets there again. Several days later, I saw they had re-worked one of the openings below the main set entrance. Another set on the steep corner of the dell had also been re-worked.

How many badgers were alive? Were they living together in the steep set or were others in use?

The precipitous approach to the set entrance in the cliff looked an impossible way down for a badger going in backwards with bedding, and it seemed likely that the bundles below the cliff had been lost on the way. Yet when I saw the quick, deft movements of the sow as she took the bedding in, I realised that this new set presented much less difficulty to her than to the watcher. Vantage-points were very scarce. I suffered hours of cramp and cold, perched as I was on a precarious ledge, having to lean to one side in an effort to conceal myself behind some scant foliage; often worried about wind direction and the possibility of being discovered by the badger should she look up and see my silhouette against the moonlit sky.

I spent many precarious and uncomfortable watches there, and my difficulties were increased by the fact that the badgers were emerging late owing to the shock of the attempted gassing. Rabbits sometimes came out first, and I think they were probably in residence before the badgers took possession. It is not unusual for rabbits to share an entrance with badgers, their burrows leading off from the side of the badgers' tunnel. No doubt it pays them to be out early.

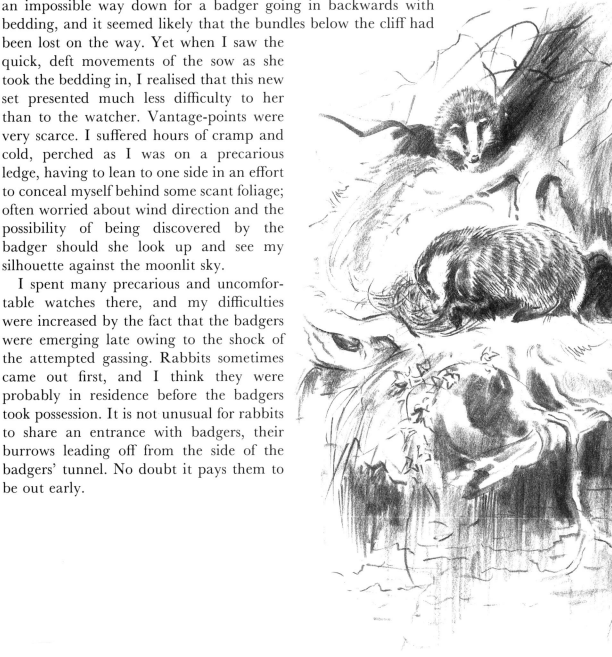

Green grass bedding was frequently taken into this set, and from later events I realised that cubs were probably there at the time and shifted to another set later. I hoped the badgers would now be left in peace, but at the end of the first week in May I found the entrance to the steep set had been stopped, and the badgers had opened a new one about twelve feet from the first.

During the next watch I heard bedding taken into the set on the sand banks. I was too far off to see the badgers there, but they sounded very busy as they journeyed to and fro to the accompaniment of the mournful cry of the peewits in nuptial flight.

That night I waited at the main set, and saw two badgers emerge. Three nights later I saw them again: a sow and a boar. They appeared to be the only inhabitants. I did not hear any sounds indicating emergence from other sets, but this did not mean that no other badgers were resident in the dell. I have often watched several leave a set and go away on their night's wandering without making any sound. Next morning I found bedding left on the path leading to the steep set, and a big bundle of bluebell flowers and foliage outside the main set. It seemed likely that badgers were occupying both sets.

A spell of bad weather brought nearly a week of heavy rain. I had been unable to go to the dell during the day before my next watch, and as I took up my stand I noticed that a tree stub previously leaning over the set entrance appeared to have subsided into it. I could not see whether the entrance was completely blocked. It was a fine evening but there was no emergence, and I could hear the badgers working inside the set in an attempt to move the stub.

The following day I found that this and an oil drum had been pushed down into the set entrance. But the badgers had made their way out over the top. In a few days' time I found that a further attempt to stop the set had been made. This explained two more fruitless watches when I had heard badgers working inside. They had at last made their way out, but it had not been easy through the tangle of roots where they had dug a new entrance beside the first. There was little sign of activity. They had evidently been given a bad scare and were keeping below ground, but in which set I could not tell.

CUBS OF THE THIRD YEAR

O N MAY 26 I WATCHED AT THE STEEP SET again, but there was no emergence. Perhaps the badgers did not fancy showing themselves on such a light and perfect evening with a full moon rising at 7.18. But I heard badgers on the sand banks below the main set, and the following evening I concealed myself behind some elder bushes to the south-east of this set. Badgers emerged from the lower opening at 9.50. They started to get bedding almost at once, and continued to bring it up to the time I left. They were collecting material from the other side of the dell, and next morning I found they had gathered grass from the headland of the cornfield. One small sample of corn had been taken and discarded; the grass was preferred. It had been torn up for a distance of seventy feet, with further cropped patches beyond. The badgers must have taken a cartload into the set that night.

In spite of this frequent renewal of bedding, I found no signs that cubs were present in either of the occupied sets. We were now in the first week of June, and my hopes of seeing cubs this year began to dwindle. With so much disturbance, and the gassing of the sets, anything might have happened, had they been expected. But on the night of June 4 I had a pleasant surprise when the sow emerged from the sandy set with three cubs.

The ground was damp, and I noticed next day that the path up to the entrance of the west set was well marked with cub spoors. Here was a new puzzle. Had the family changed over to this set during the night or had they merely visited there? Could it be that there was more than one family? This seemed too much to hope for. That evening I watched the sandy set again, and saw nothing till 10.30. The sow came out first and returned, apparently to say the coast was clear, then the whole family, including the boar, followed.

Coronation fireworks displays started immediately in the villages north and south, about a mile and a half away. I thought this would mean the end of watching for the night, but to my surprise only one cub returned to the set. He was in no hurry, and was soon out again. I could hear the family wandering about at the bottom of the dell, unconcerned, while Roman candles, rockets. and other spluttering devices shrieked their way up into the sky, frightening every domestic animal within miles. The badgers made no attempt to come back to the set, but went away on a foraging expedition.

My next watch was enlivened by loud dance music from the village green, where other Coronation festivities were being held. But emergence was about the usual time. The cubs were very entertaining as they accompanied the parents who were bringing bedding along the path below me. The sow came with her bundle, a little cub trotting along in front; the bedding was taken in, and the sow appeared again, followed by the playful cub. The boar also took part in the work which now started in earnest. The adults came up the path repeatedly with their loads, the cubs running beside them, having the appearance of thoroughly enjoying the proceedings. They were bubbling over with excitement, squeaking and yelping as they played; getting in the way of the parents; running on ahead; returning to them, then back to the set as though the whole business was proceeding at much too slow a pace for their liking.

The path below the oak was busy again next evening when the sow, boar, and cubs were making frequent use of it. The cubs were at play there, and I had a clear view from the top of the bank.

They would face one another with heads lowered, dodging from side to side, thrusting with their little snouts till one made a dart at his opponent, to twist round in a flash and come back again to the attack. This would go on till it ended in one of the cubs suddenly racing up the bank with the rest scrambling after. A wild chase followed, then the game would start afresh.

I was watching this set one evening when I saw, for the first time, badgers emerging from the chalk set, west. Unfortunately, it was about thirty feet away, but I was able to see a sow and boar with three cubs at the entrance, for the time was only 9.35, and the light was very good.

I did not see any badgers emerge from the sandy set that night. Again I wondered whether they had moved to the chalk set. An indication that this might be the case was the fact that inspection, next day, of the latrine previously used by badgers from the sandy set showed that it had not been used the night before.

The next evening I saw the two adults and three cubs again emerge from the chalk set in good light. After they had left I heard badgers on the path leading to the sandy set. As the cubs I had been watching were moving around, it was impossible to say whether some of their number had gone to the sandy set, or whether, by good fortune, there was another family.

The following night the boar emerged from the chalk set at 9.10. I had a wonderful view in full daylight, and stood with bated breath least he should see me through my scanty covering of foliage. I noted light streaks in the fur along his back, which might be a useful aid to his identification in the future. This was a promising start to the evening's watching.

He made his way cautiously up the path beside the set, and the sow's face appeared at the entrance, but it was quickly lost in the sudden scuffle as the boar, who had turned round in a flash, scrambled down the set. He had evidently heard or scented something he did not like. In a few minutes two rabbits came down the bank beside me at breakneck pace. They halted a second to give their warning thumps on the ground at the entrance to their burrow, and were gone! The intruder that scared the badger must have been on their trail, though I saw nothing of it.

While watching the chalk set two nights later, I again heard badgers on the path leading to the sandy set, and on June 25 there was so much noise on the sand banks that I made my way to the oak overlooking the path. I had not been there long when two cubs came up the bank to play round my feet. Seeing them very near, I realised at once that they were smaller than the cubs from the chalk set, and this was another family. There was a lot of play that night, and the activity on the sand banks worked up into a frenzied game in which the cubs finally rushed along the path to the bottom of the dell. Whether they were joined by the cubs from the chalk set I could not tell, but the noisiness of the party suggested that more than the little fellows from the sandy set were playing.

At one time it seemed as though a small hurricane had hit the elder bushes and nettles. The cubs were chasing one another through the undergrowth, and I could hear the incessant thud of little paws as they went round and round and up and over the hummock to scramble along the fallen tree, and off again in another race. Most of this was in silence, but every now and again excited little yelps could be heard as the play reached a fresh pitch of exuberance.

The badgers were emerging early and were usually out before 9 p.m. which gave me some good opportunities for sketching. But one evening I waited at the chalk set hopefully, and there was no

emergence. About 10 o'clock I heard badgers coming down the path from the sandy set behind me. A sow and cub crossed the hummock and took the path to the chalk set. The sow went to the entrance and looked down with the air of one who has come to call and found no one at home.

The relative sizes of cubs are often difficult to define in the half-light, but I had the impression that this was one of the bigger cubs and the sow from the chalk set. The set seemed deserted, and though I had no proof, I thought the family had probably spent the day with the badgers in the sandy set. This was not the only time when I felt one of the family had shared a day with another.

I had many enjoyable evenings watching and sketching the two families, but I felt the need of a better position where I could get a clearer view of the badgers in the sandy set. They were inclined to go down through the bottom of the dell, and leave me listening to their wanderings and play as I stood on top of the bank. I set to work to clear a path through the foot of the dell, along which it would be possible to get away quietly. This was a considerable task as I had to trim the elder bushes to make a tunnel through them to a position below the set. The brushwood there gave cover and a fallen tree was conveniently placed for a weary watcher to lean against. Beyond this tunnel I had also to rake a way clear of fallen leaves and twigs along which I could get out to the field on the north side of the dell. This done, I enlisted the help of two companions who had long suffered my enthusiasm, for I had recently noticed that a third set appeared to be in use on the north-east corner, and I wanted to make a count of the badgers.

Nothing was seen at this set, but the family from the chalk set, west, were out early in the cornfield. The third entrance to the set was in sand, and the cubs would go down into it and come up to fling sand vigorously out of their coats in all directions, suggesting they had been enjoying a roll. This entrance to the set was a popular playground and the steep little bank down into the cornfield offered temptation to the mischievous cub who waited his opportunity to thrust his nose under a playmate's tummy and send him rolling into the thistles below.

The watcher there saw an amusing interlude when a venturesome, small cub from the sandy set came running along the path, and hurried down the entrance. Apparently he came to call, but finding no one in, scrambled out to run across to the chalk opening. He seemed to fare better at this one for he did not come out again. Let us hope he found as pleasant a welcome as Kenneth Grahame's Moley.

Watching at the sandy set, I had an entertaining evening. The cubs appeared very self-possessed till a blackbird flew shrieking through the bushes in alarm. They made a dive for the set, but were out again in no time. Full of play, they faced one another, dodging this way and that with heads lowered, then one made a rush at his opponent, bowling him over. There was a quick turn round, and they were facing again. This time a sudden rush ended in leap-frog as the attacking cub, finding his way barred by his brother, leapt over his back. Next began a game in which one continually thrust at the other, bowling him down the set, and tumbling after. They were gone only a few seconds, and up they came; then down again in the same way, disappearing and reappearing like little Jack-in-the-box figures. I wondered how they made such a quick turn round in the confined space of the set entrance.

They kept this game up till the sow emerged with a third cub, and the fun began all over again. There were tremendous rushes and scuffles that often took all three cubs up to the top of the bank and round the bushes there, to come sliding head-over-heels in a wild scramble that I thought, many times, must end in their rolling down the bank to my feet. But they were wonderfully agile, and always managed to collect themselves and scramble back to the path in time. They seemed, also, to enjoy slithering down the steepest part of the bank when they made no attempt to stop themselves.

At last the game quietened down, and one of the cubs found a new diversion in digging out a rabbit hole below the set entrance. He clawed vigorously at the sand and chalk that rattled down the slope to my feet, making him turn round and stare as though wondering whether it was possible he could be making all that noise, or could there be a bogey of the dark down there. I began to feel guilty hidden in my retreat of shadows.

Another cub was sitting on the ledge above. An idea seemed to seize the digger. He scrambled up to the cub; rushed down to his hole, and started scratching out the sand again; up to the cub, down to his hole, up again, and so on till it could almost have been supposed that he was trying to induce the other cub to come down to look at his work. At last he succeeded, and together they examined the hole. The digger now seemed content. He left his work, and another game of chase started and went on till the badgers finally dispersed, giving me a chance to get away undetected.

A SEASONAL MOVE

THERE WERE NOW ELEVEN BADGERS IN THE DELL, with a possible twelve, as four cubs had been seen several times at the chalk set, west. The more usual number of three there suggested the possibility that one of the four might be a visitor from the other set.

As three of the 1951 cubs were still in residence with the original pair last autumn, it would seem that two had left, or been killed by the gassing, and one mated female remained, subsequently, to give birth to cubs.

The next evening I watched below the sandy set again, as I hoped early emergence would give me a chance of some sketching. But when I arrived two rabbiting dogs at the west end of the dell made so much noise that I was obliged to leave my position in the hope of chasing them off. When I arrived on the scene, peace reigned, and there was no sign of them. I could well imagine them lying behind the bushes, grinning broadly, their sandy tongues hanging out, their sides heaving; glad of the opportunity to get their breath while I looked for them in vain. As I arrived back at the sandy set, the barking began afresh. Although a dog-lover, I wished them somewhere else.

Emergence was delayed, but there was a lot of play among the cubs when they did come out, and the scent from the musk glands was very noticeable. The emission of scent is said to be caused by excitement, but in this instance it was very evident as the cubs emerged, and before play started. Unlike that of some members of the family *Mustelidae* the badger's scent is not objectionable to man. I have noticed it on a number of occasions before the badgers leave the set, and have found it to be a reliable indication that they are about to emerge. The glands are also used for laying scent, which the badgers leave on a stone or other suitable object along their paths.

On the following night I was able to make a certain count of four cubs playing at the sandy set. I could see them running along the top of the slopes, against the light, and many times they came almost to my feet as they rolled together down the bank. The speed and vigour with which they scrambled up again were a joy to watch. Through all the games they were practically silent, but I could hear the excited yelps of the other family on the edge of the cornfield.

Only a low flying aircraft distracted the cubs from play. Two were at the set entrance as the plane went over, and they stopped playing to stare into the darkness for a moment, then tumbled over one another to get down the set. This was the first time I had seen badgers take notice of aircraft. They were out again as soon as it had passed.

The next morning I found there had been great activity at the chalk set, west. The sandy opening had also been re-worked, and cub spoors showed clearly everywhere in the newly turned out sand. Bedding was left outside the chalk entrance, and there had been further work on the opening at the edge of the cornfield. It was notable that sets were being re-worked all over the dell.

The next night, six badgers emerged from the sandy set. This verified my count of four cubs there the night before. The sow and boar were also seen. The first cub was out at 9.8. It was soon followed by the rest of the family. There was a lot of play which, as usual, was very entertaining to watch. The chasing and scuffling became faster and faster as the cubs rushed up and down the banks at great speed. They often came down with such impetus that their efforts to stop suddenly would swing them round in a half-circle, their actions resembling those of a skier pulling out of a run.

The sand banks provided many an evening's entertainment, but these hilarious exhibitions of play did not always occur. Sometimes there was no game at all, and the badgers would go away along the hedge towards the farm, or out into the field to forage. It was impossible to say what governed their actions, and why there should be so much play sometimes and at other times all attention given to the more serious business of feeding without delay.

On July 24 I found that the entrance on the edge of the cornfield and the playground by it showed signs of being very much in use. This, I thought, would be a place worth watching, for the light was good there. I made plans to watch standing in the hedge about ten feet from the set. A tree stub was conveniently placed to give me a good vantage-point that overlooked a considerable area of the cornfield.

I arrived at 8.30 and climbed into my eyrie in the hedge to wait, sketch-book in hand. The cubs came to the set entrance at 9.30, but went back. They appeared again in ten minutes' time, but full emergence was not till 10 o'clock. Three cubs and two adults came out, and there was a lot of play on the flattened area at the edge of the field. The play of the cubs expressed the joy known only to the little young things of the world; joy as yet unspoiled by the realisation of fear and danger. It was a saddening thought that such happiness is often extinguished by man's hasty use of his power over animals.

My pleasure in watching was tempered by misgivings when I saw that some of the corn had been flattened. The damage did not amount to much, as the crop there was poor under the trees, and full of thistles. I hoped the farmer would take the badgers' intrusion in good part, and remember the beneficial work they were doing all through the year.

The next evening they were busy around the entrance by the cornfield. The sow and boar were bringing bedding from the grass bank, and taking it into the set through the chalk entrance. Five cubs were at play in good light, and it was evident they had visitors from the sandy set. The sow emerged that night in apparently carefree mood, rolling and playing with the cubs who appeared at times as a jumbled mass of fur while they tussled together just below me.

The view from the hedge was well worth the discomfort of standing in the tree stub, but after two nights' watching there with my feet at an acute angle, the tree having been cut off on the slant, I made a small sawdust pad to stand on. The stuffing could be adjusted to make an uneven surface level, and it served me in good stead in the future on many a rugged foothold.

From this position I was able to get some useful sketching, particularly when the badgers came out in good light. One evening a muddy-nosed cub emerged in full daylight; he looked the complete little ruffian with strands of bedding across his nose. I hoped he would stay above ground and be followed by the others, but after a while, as though feeling peckish, he took a mouthful of herbage and retired underground with it.

Badgers do not emerge muddy. They keep themselves remarkably clean by grooming. I have watched a family of half a dozen all busily licking each other's fur, though they already looked in such perfect condition that further grooming appeared unnecessary. The sow is often seen grooming the young cubs, for her attention to their cleanliness is meticulous. At the time when the badgers were going into the cornfield to feed, the fallen tree where they cleaned their claws came in for a lot of attention, and showed fresh claw marks daily.

There was now an interesting change in the population of the dell. On August 6 the corn was cut, and that night, though the badgers emerged from the sandy set at about the usual time, there was no play, and only one emerged from the chalk set, west, very late.

The next night there was a lot of play on the sand banks, and later at the north-east corner. It seemed that the harvesting had driven the badgers away from the west end of the dell. None was heard to come from the chalk set, west, and I thought the family had probably gone to the north-east corner, but this theory was later proved wrong.

I was expecting a seasonal move on the part of both families, for according to Ernest Neal's August records badgers tend to leave their sets and congregate in large sets together at this time of year. The sandy set and the set on the north-east corner were both being cleared out, and paths led down to a newly made playground below the steep cliff. A path went up the opposite bank towards the playing tree above the sandy set, suggesting a connection between the two.

There were signs of great activity around the newly occupied set on the north-east corner, and observation in daylight influenced me in watching there where I thought the two families might be in residence together. It was exasperating to hear emergence from the sandy set while no badgers came out from the set on the corner.

But it was not long before I saw some of the cubs racing along the field at the top of the chalk cliff, and presently they were playing all round me. This happened on a number of occasions: the badgers would emerge from the sandy set, and come to play by the one on the north-east corner. Yet there were never more than six present, and I realised with great regret that the cornfield family had left the dell. I had no evidence of their being in any set after the night following the harvesting.

MOONLIT GRASS

THE EVENINGS WERE DRAWING IN, WHICH MADE observation of the sandy sets difficult, for they were heavily overshadowed. The badgers were restless, and it was never possible to tell from which set they would come. With more light on the north-east corner I often watched there. But the badgers played a game of hide-and-seek with me, sometimes emerging from the sandy set and sometimes from the corner.

The sow was already busying herself in preparation for the winter, and I watched her working on the sandy set for a long time one evening. She sent a shower of stones and sand down on my feet as she cleared the entrance. After this she went into the set and there was a silent period till she came up again with more soil and discarded bedding. She made many journeys, always remaining below long enough to indicate that she was bringing her load from some distance underground.

I followed the badgers' path out of the dell and across the fields by daylight. Cowcakes had been turned over, and moles unearthed on the way. The path led through a hedge and went into a cornfield not yet harvested. There was also a flattened playground in the grass under the hedge.

One evening I tried the experiment of following the badgers out there in the moonlight. The wind was in my favour and I was able to get very near, as they were making a lot of noise under the hedges. The moon also gave me many good views of the cubs at play on top of the chalk cliff where they were in the open field.

It was possible to find positions on the edge of the dell where, with the dark background of trees, the scanty cover of foliage was

enough to conceal the watcher in the shadows, and there I was able to observe, very intimately, some of the actions of the badgers in the moonlight. It was interesting to see the thorough way in which the foraging sow searched the grass, alternately thrusting the snout down to the turf and lifting up over the grass in regular sequence as she moved forward.

With a desire to get nearer to the badgers in the field above the cliff, I made a foothold in the trees' roots on a narrow ledge where I could get a ringside view. The four cubs often played there only a few feet away. They spent most of their time in play, but sometimes one would detach herself from the rest, and try the experiment of collecting bedding. She made a half-hearted job of it, pulling up a few mouthfuls of grass which she gathered into a ball and brought to within several feet of the set entrance where the temptation to join in the play invariably proved too much for her.

The cubs seemed overjoyed at the freedom of the field, which must have appeared to them as a tremendous open space after the confines of the sets and the dell where they usually played. Every now and then one would express his feelings by leaping into the air, all four feet off the ground at once, as a young lamb in spring. And when play was over, they raced off at speed, making wide circles through the grass on their way to the tree-topped ridge that crossed the pasture.

Their choice of the field as a playground was a great advantage, as the light there was much better than inside the dell. I had many enjoyable evenings on the cliff top till west and south-west winds forced me to take to the nettle patch on the north. This, too, had to be abandoned, as I felt that the watcher's silhouette would be seen against the sky, and I wanted to avoid disturbing the badgers. They seemed to have settled down at last.

They remained in the set on the north-east corner for just over three weeks, but on the night of September 3 a great quantity of bedding was taken into the sandy set. I left the cliff top, and under cover of the noise the badgers were making I was able to approach the hedge and watch them pulling the sere grass in the field. They lunged at it to get a grip with the teeth, then pulled it with such force that at times the upward jerks took their front legs off the ground. They put great energy into the job, and the noise of the wrenching and tugging and the carrying away of many bundles could be heard clearly from a distance of a hundred yards.

The next night they emerged from the sandy set. I was waiting on the cliff by the north-east corner. Though they came across and played on the field close by, they soon went away and left me with only the wood-mice for company. Numbers of them sat up in the branches of the hawthorns bordering the field, to feast on the ripening haws. It was rarely possible to see them, but their busy little jaws were heard munching from dusk onwards.

THE END OF SUMMER

THE BADGERS WERE STILL IN THE SANDY SET, BUT they usually came to the north-east corner where it was lighter. As the evenings were drawing in I decided to watch there one night, and I was lucky.

It was not long before a cub came out of the spinney and ran past me to the corner set. She soon trotted out again, and sat on the path. I could have bent down and touched her as she sat listening, ears erect, head up, to the sounds of dogs, and people talking on the other side of the field. The wind was right, and the cub remained for some time blissfully unaware that I was standing just behind her.

Eventually she wandered back to the spinney where she could be heard eating acorns, but seeking bigger fry, she ran out to the field again. After a short time she came back and laid something on the path a few feet from me, and began to eat it. Next morning, examination of the ground where she had been feeding revealed scraps of moleskin, but I could not see what she had brought in the half-light. The appalling stench that came up told me only that it was something that had been dead a very long time. I had always understood that badgers would not touch carrion, but there was no doubt concerning the nature of this.

The cub began to scrape the mole this way and that with her claws, before starting to tear at the flesh, eating with noisy relish. Unable to see the size of the meal clearly, I thought, from the loud cracking of bones, that something much larger than a mole was being devoured.

Every now and then the badger would stop eating to scrape the mole again, and in doing so pulled it backwards a few feet with a similar action to that used when taking in bedding. In this way she gradually retreated to the mouth of the near-by set, from where I could hear the loud crunch of bones between halts for more scraping. The backward movements gradually took the cub past the set opening, and up on the field beyond, where she finished her meal. She then returned, snuffing the ground, and came to the place where she had first laid the mole; there a few scraps were found and relished. The appalling smell still clung to the badger's fur as she trotted off hopefully over the pasture to the place where she had discovered her prize.

Eating the mole took nearly a quarter of an hour, which seemed a long time for such a small meal. The three other cubs were around the set entrance at the time, but there was no interference from them.

The study of dung analysis has thrown much light on the question of what badgers eat, but it does not tell all the story. If we could follow them about and see them eating we could learn more. I have wondered whether a badger sometimes gets a taste for a kind of food and will search for that only. I have found dung containing the elytra of dozens of beetles, and it is difficult to understand how so many could have been found at one time.

Diet is, of course, seasonal; the badger must take what he can get. Herbage is eaten most of the year around. Acorns, beech, mast, blackberries, and other wild fruits are all taken in season and supplemented with earthworms, grubs, and small mammals when available. Towards the end of summer I found many places where moles had been caught in the pasture, and I frequently came across holes where the badgers had unearthed them, sometimes from their 'untitumps' and sometimes from their runs. Many of these holes were about six inches across and five deep, and were clearly the work of the badger's claws; others were made at intervals along the runs and were not more than two inches across, tapering to about an inch. They were neat and round, and without doubt made by the badger's nose thrusting down into the runs in search of insects.

Late in September and at the beginning of October there was a great concentration of mice in the stubble field. Many nests were turned out, and holes excavated. The badgers did useful work in this way, for it seemed that any mouse or vole that attempted to set up residence in or near the dell was doomed to a short life.

1953

Before this the badgers had gone through a very quiet period. They would emerge and go away in search of food without any preliminary play. I have often noticed these quiet spells, and found that they usually occur when food is scarce owing to dry weather.

The dell badgers had a chosen area of paths around the set they occupied. It was not necessarily the same with each occupation of the set. When they were in the sandy set earlier in the year they always went out by the path leading down to the bottom of the dell, and it was there they played before going along the hedge. Since they had returned to this set they were coming up on top to forage in the spinney, and go out into the field on the south side. I have also noticed a tendency for the badgers to go and visit and play around the set they have recently vacated. They will do this for several nights, after which they desert it entirely.

I had contemplated being able to make some clear observations during the period leading up to the full moon, for though badgers are often shy of coming into the brilliant light, they can be seen well when the moon is less than full or screened by light cloud. I had looked forward hopefully to this after a period of intense darkness during the first two weeks in September. I had to feel my way out of the dell on these occasions, and anyone with me kept a hand on my coat for fear of being lost! I usually acted as pilot, for, by now, I was on intimate terms with most of the trees and bushes in the dell.

The weather marred several watches when the moon should have been at its best. One night I stood out for some time in pouring rain. The sounds from the badgers ceased as it started, and I heard no more of them. In the end I, too, made for home. The rain cleared later, and next morning I went to the dell as the damp soil was likely to give a very good indication of the badgers' movements of the night before. The most frequented place was by the chalk set, west. The sandy entrance to this set and the bank around it showed many spoors. The chalk entrance had been freshly worked for the first time since the set was vacated in August, and the cornfield opening was being used.

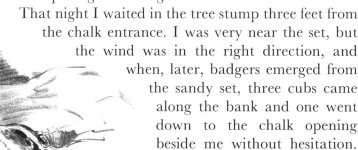

That night I waited in the tree stump three feet from the chalk entrance. I was very near the set, but the wind was in the right direction, and when, later, badgers emerged from the sandy set, three cubs came along the bank and one went down to the chalk opening beside me without hesitation.

There he met another cub coming out of the set, and appeared to greet it, as their noses met. It was one of the family who had spent the night in this set. As the cub reached the top of the bank it was met by another, who, as the first had done, greeted it nose to nose in salutation.

Play then started, and the cubs raced along the path between the sets, backwards and forwards, panting like little steam engines as they came, pausing for breath in a sudden silence or to climb the trunk of the big oak tree. I saw one cling with all four paws to the trunk till another cub gave him a push, and down he slid. Badgers enjoy climbing, but I do not think they can climb far on an upright trunk; probably the most they can manage is about a foot from the ground, but where a tree is sloping, I believe they will climb till they are ten feet or more above the ground. On the hummock there was an arm of the fallen tree half buried in sand. It leant over at an acute angle, and was a favourite climbing place for the badgers. Their claw marks could be seen along its full length.

So much interest was now being shown in the chalk set, west, that I thought there would soon be a change to this from the sandy set. The sow, repeatedly, went in and out, and at last took herself off in search of bedding. I heard her bringing it back noisily through the bushes, but a sudden shower of rain made her drop the bundle and seek shelter.

I and another enthusiast watched for a long time that night. The badgers, who were soon out again after the rain, were around us most of the time. One cub frequently came to the chalk opening and passed many times within a foot of my companion. Later he came and sat by the tree, had a long sniff at our boots, then, after gazing up at us for a time, trotted back to the set. He was a little puzzled, but unafraid. Even the sow, always the most sensitive, failed to detect us, and came snuffing and grunting her way down to the oak near-by, where she poked her nose into every hollow under the roots in search of beetles.

On the night of September 28 many journeys were made to fetch bedding to the west set and the sandy set where the badgers were still in residence. As usual, great energy was put into the job. They were taking the sere tops of the grass on a bank bordering the stubble field, as I lay for a while under the stars listening and enjoying this time taken in truancy from my own world.

The badgers were very noisy in their work. I could imagine a timid person, on her way across the fields, beating a hasty retreat with the thought that some nefarious business was going on late at night.

And how industrious the animals are on those nights of bedding changes. Never pausing, they hurry out of the sets for more again and again, as though the job has to be done, like our spring cleaning, and the sooner it is finished the better.

It is difficult to realise how alive the countryside is at night unless one goes out to listen. Leaving the working badger unheard, I made my way as silently as possible across the fields. I stopped to listen to the innumerable rustlings in the hedges; the squeaking rats and other small creatures; the call of the moorhen; the owls, and around the farm the symphony of many grasshoppers.

During one October morning I put down some acorns in heaps on the path above the sandy set, as I wanted to make some sketches of badgers feeding. They were heard everywhere else in the dell, and emerged from the north-east corner. This indicated a possible change-over to the corner set, and I was prompted to try there next night. But, the badgers were back again in the sandy set, and I heard an acorn feast going on above it. To reach the area was practically impossible owing to dry leaves underfoot, and had I arrived on the scene I should have seen little as the night was very dark.

The following morning I found that the acorns had been taken from each of the heaps I had put down, and I hastily renewed the supply.

That night the sky cleared, and gave more light. I stood in the hazel bush above the sandy set, with tempting heaps of acorns on the path two feet away. I heard badgers emerging from the corner set at 6 o'clock, and others were out of the sandy set a few minutes later. I had to listen patiently to a bout of scratching at the set entrance where it was too dark to see the badgers clearly, but very soon one cub came up on top of the bank and discovered a heap of acorns. She started to eat at once, sitting down to the job, and busily chewing as though ravenous after the day's rest. It was not difficult to count the number she ate, each one being first loudly cracked, then chewed for some time. When she had eaten about thirty acorns, she was joined by a second badger. If I had not been able to see the relative sizes, I could still have told that this was an adult by the marked difference in the sounds of chewing which were decidedly adult compared with the timing of smaller jaws of the cub.

A third badger now joined the party, and the adult left the cub's heap for a larger one beside it. What a feast there was, eclipsing any I had heard on similar nights last year when the badgers had to search for the acorns one by one in the undergrowth. As on those occasions, scratching was a feature, and one that failed to interrupt the continuous chewing which was very rapid and not unlike the sound made by the lapping of thirsty puppies.

The two cubs at last finished their meal, and wandered away, but the adult went on eating for over half an hour. Towards the end of the meal the jaws began to tire, and the chewing became slower and slower. At last there was a pause, and it seemed the limit had been reached. I heard a satisfied snort and a sigh. Was the meal ended? No, one more acorn could be managed with an effort. There was a short silence, and yet another was found and chewed. A pause again, and another eaten. This went on for a while longer, then, with a loud hiccup, the badger disappeared down the bank.

I made my way out of the dell, any rustles from dry leaves underfoot being covered by the noisy cracking of more acorns, for the feast was still going on farther down the path.

THE LEAN DAYS

IT WAS NOW LATE IN OCTOBER AND THE BADGERS were getting more difficult to observe, but the evenings were warm, and they would sometimes remain for long periods near the sets, quietly surveying the scene in restful mood as though, their work of rearing a family over, they felt entitled to some leisure.

During these long quiet periods it was difficult for the watcher to move away without causing disturbance, which was something I always tried to avoid. But on the night of October 19 the boar and sow sat so long by the cornfield entrance, that I was at last obliged to leave while they were there. I had moved to this set from another where I had failed to see emergence, and as I reached the cover of the hedge, I saw that two badgers were sitting on the bank below me only a few feet away. They carried on a mumbled conversation in low tones, and occasionally the boar would wander out on the field to tear up a few mouthfuls of bedding that he brought to the sow, as though suggesting she should take it into the set. But she was in no mood for work. Perhaps she felt she had made enough beds for the year, and nothing was going to interrupt her well-earned rest.

The badgers were still there after an hour and a quarter when, being tied for time, I was forced to leave. The wind was in my favour, and as I crept almost inch by inch, I heard them mumbling together contentedly, oblivious of my going.

I planned to make, in the coming months, the closest winter watch I had yet kept, and set myself the task of going to the dell every night that the weather did not make watching impracticable.

The sets were a car journey from my home, and the fogs gave some trouble. At times I started out only to be turned back by a thick blanket of fog, but when it was at all possible to get through I did so. Rain sometimes sent the badgers in and drove me away, but the late October moon gave me a chance with some clear nights. On such a night, having been disappointed through no badgers emerging at the set I watched, I crept out to wait by the hawthorns on top of the north bank. Here I hoped to see the badgers foraging in the field, for I could hear plenty of activity in and around the dell.

It was not long before three cubs came from the direction of the north-east corner set, and two adults out from the dell to my left.

The cubs came down the path towards me eating acorns on the way, and the adults foraged and snuffled noisily in the grass, undeterred by the bright moonlight.

In my experience, badgers are not necessarily alerted by the alarm of a companion. I knew, as the cubs came nearer, that my luck was to be short-lived, for I was not well hidden by the sparse cover of the hawthorns. Soon the foremost cub was within a foot of my tree, and I was discovered. The young badger froze instantly and looked up at me, then raced at top speed for the set. The others stared after him with an expression that seemed to say, "What's bitten him?" and went on eating. They finally wandered away without suspecting that they were being watched.

At times the close proximity of the unsuspicious badger is incredible. On one occasion when waiting on the precipice near the north-east corner set I came almost nose to nose with a badger without his discovering me. I was standing, as I often did, half-way down the cliff where only my head and shoulders came above the level of the field. I had put down acorns early in the day, tucking some into the hollows of roots of the hawthorns there, though I hardly dared to hope that any badger would get as near without scenting me. Yet when one did emerge, it sat eating acorns only an arm's length away. Presently it came snuffling around the hawthorn roots until its snout was little more than a foot from my face, yet I was not discovered.

I watched on most nights through November, often waiting for hours in the bitter cold with one eye on the fog, the motorist's nightmare that was gradually closing down. I often started out in fair weather that turned to foul, and staggered home through soaking wet fields, falling down rabbit holes in the dark, stumbling into bogs, getting entangled in barbed wire and bramble thickets, and on one occasion even coming near to being shot.

Watching down the bank of the dell, I heard what I took to be back-firing from a car in trouble, for it was a dark night and there seemed little likelihood that anyone would be out with a gun. I had forgotten the modern 'sport' of rabbit shooting by the light of headlamps. With my mind very much on the badgers I ignored report after report, and it was not till I heard shot falling around me that I realised what was happening.

There was plenty of activity on the part of the badgers throughout November. Bedding was taken in and a lot of soil turned out from the two occupied sets. The cubs were still playful and very noisy when they were not subdued by bad weather. The usual playing tree and another were much used. On my frequent

daylight visits I noticed that the fallen tree across the bed of the pool always showed fresh claw marks, and it seemed the badgers must go there every night, or I should say, every morning, for there was no doubt that they went to the tree to clean their claws before retiring into the sets at dawn.

December 1953 was exceptionally warm. I had never seen so much sign of activity at this time of year before. The soil, being damp, defined paths very clearly, and areas around the sets and playing trees were pounded flat with activity, while the dell showed evidence of rooting for mice, moles, and other small fry from end to end. The badgers were also seeking food among the clover that covered the stubble field, and no doubt they found plenty of grubs, earthworms, and slugs under the wet leaves in such mild weather. During the second week in December manure from a poultry farm was spread on this field, and with it a number of dead chickens in varying stages of decay. It was not long before I found evidence of some of the dead birds being eaten. The fact that the badger will take dead meat shows how easily he can be convicted when entirely innocent of the kill. Too many people are ready to jump to conclusions, and for those who wish to condemn him the fact of his eating a victim is enough. Badgers had been in the dell for many years and poultry had been kept in safety and continued to be kept in safety no more than a field away.

The pasture was to be ploughed this autumn, and preliminary work started on December 23 when the overhanging trees bordering the badgers' haunt were cut back, and the thicket of brambles and wild rose on the south boundary, where the badgers used to root, and sometimes had their latrine, was cut away. This drove them from their paths on that side of the dell, but they continued to be active at the sand bank set not far off. An old oil drum that had partially blocked the entrance for a long time had recently been moved and I hoped that the badgers would be encouraged to use this opening, for it was the easiest to watch closely. This they obligingly did, turning out great quantities of sand during the next few nights.

Perhaps the greatest difficulty that besets the badger-watcher in winter is the fact that the animals often emerge long after dark, and to be sure of getting into position quietly one should be at the chosen spot while the evening is still light enough to show twigs and other tell-tale objects underfoot.

Times of emergence were now very irregular, and I had several lengthy waits in vain. I decided to put in a watch from 4.45 and stay as long as I could bear the cold. If the badgers had not emerged when I left, I would try getting into position from that time the next night. I waited till 7.30 and no badger stirred. It was a bitter moonlit night with a cruel east wind, and I was just about as cold as I could be. I hurried home cheerfully with the thought of making my way into the dell tomorrow evening by the light of the moon.

But heavy cloud, rain and fog spoiled my chances for the next three nights. Then, on December 20, came a clear sky with the full moon. I ignored the slight ground mist, and started out, but I had not gone far when I realised I should have to turn back, for I met what proved to be one of the thickest fogs of the year.

After this the weather made watching impossible for a week. By then the moon was rising too late to be of any help in getting into the dell. But in spite of this I was determined to try. Having failed to see the badgers on my last watch, I arrived at 7.15 and timed my waiting well for they emerged at 7.50. The following night I was not so lucky, and when I arrived at 7.30 the badgers were already out. Yet by waiting patiently till they had left the set, I was able to get into a good position above the sand bank, and witnessed a busy evening that included the bringing of bedding to the main set. There was a lot of play and 'talking' among the cubs which were still with the parents through the winter.

We were now at the end of December and the badgers were in no way inactive through the very cold weather that had brought winter in at last. The grass, that night, was heavily frosted as I made my way home, and I decided to try the experiment of putting out food for the badgers, for it seemed they were probably having a lean time.

FINDINGS FOR THE YEAR 1953

Of the five badgers resident in the dell for the past two years only the original pair and one cub remained. This cub was paired with a visiting boar who was resident with her throughout the summer. It was not possible to say what had befallen the other two cubs. They may have left to join other colonies, or been killed by the gassing.

Four cubs were born to the original pair, and three to the paired cub. It was estimated that the three were born several weeks earlier than the other family. The original pair resident in the sand banks were noticed to emerge later than the others. The latter, having spent the early spring in the set on the chalk cliff, moved to the west end of the dell later.

The friendly nature of the two families was noted, and there were times when they visited each other, sometimes spending a day together. The family at the west end left the dell on the night following the cutting of the corn over the set, and were not seen again.

It was learned that badgers, contrary to belief, will eat carrion.

Exceptionally warm weather in December made the badgers more active than I have ever known them to be at that time of year. There was also activity in the bitter weather that followed, the badgers coming out even during the severe frosts and snow.

FIRST ADVENTURE

EARLY JANUARY BROUGHT THE WORST WEATHER of the winter, and in addition to acorns collected in the autumn, I put out chestnuts, apples, carrots, cheese, bread, potatoes, and turnips. I hoped these would help to take the edge off the badgers' appetites.

The weather was still bitterly cold by the middle of the month, and I was supplying food every day. Chestnuts proved to be the badgers' favourite. Potatoes and turnips were never touched, cooked or raw. All the food disappeared, and a proportion was, no doubt, taken by other animals and birds. A lone robin always followed me through the dell and openly enjoyed his share, but I had a strong suspicion that a horde of other birds watched the proceedings from a distance and descended on the feast as soon as my back was turned.

During January the badgers made a new opening to the north-east set, coming out in the pasture about twenty feet from the main entrance. This promised an unobstructed view of any animals emerging there, but signs that a set had received attention overnight may not mean that badgers are at home when we come to watch there in the evening. In fact the only way to be sure of this is to see the badgers return by dawn. But it is no easy task to be up before dawn every morning.

The entry in my diary for January 11 records a night of brilliant moonlight, and I was able to see five badgers out together on the sand banks. During the summer there had been six in the family, and it seemed likely that one male cub had left in the autumn, and here were three female cubs with the two adults. It was a cold and windy night with frost, and these factors with bright moonlight made the badgers furtive, though I was able to note some interesting positions before some dispersed and others retired back into the set.

That night I witnessed a marked contrast in different badgers' sense of smell. When I arrived at 7.30 I went to the cover of the hazel, west of the set, for I had heard badgers out, and felt there was too much risk in trying to get into the more exposed position in the tree above the sand banks. But after a while their sounds ceased; they all seemed to have left the area, and I decided to attempt a change-over to the tree. I got there successfully but only just in time, for in a few minutes the sow emerged from the main set. She went towards the hazel I had just left, but stopped dead a yard from where I had stood, then turned and raced for the set. Apparently she had scented me. Yet later in the evening when two cubs emerged from the main entrance and came along the path beside me, one actually snuffed the step down the bank where I had been obliged to tread to reach the tree, but she did not scent me, and came into the space between the brushwood where I had climbed up. I was standing no more than a foot above her. She sat for some minutes overlooking the dell below, then suddenly turned away, knocking her head with a resounding crack on a low branch. I thought she must have realised my presence, but she sat on the path apparently unperturbed for a while before making her way back to the set.

Another time I was watching in the same position with a strong north wind taking my scent across the path when two of the previous year's cubs came along it. One passed by and the other took several minutes to detect the scent. These instances suggest that the cubs may not have the badger's highly developed sense of smell until they are mature. It is known that this sense is more marked in the sow than in the boar, particularly when she has the need to protect her cubs.

Bitter weather continued through January and into February. Most of the time the ground was frozen hard, and I wondered how the badgers managed to get enough to eat. It was a task to keep up my contributions, but I went to the dell every day with chestnuts and other food.

The badgers remained active all the time in spite of severe frosts of over 20°F. On several nights bedding was taken to the sandy and north-east corner sets. Frozen grass was of little use, and I noticed that straw had been gathered from the edge of the stubble field and taken to the corner set, while the badgers from the sand banks had been reduced to scraping up what little moss they could find in the bottom of the dell.

I now added clover hay for bedding to my daily load of food, and the badgers made use of it the first night. On the morning of February 1, when there had been a light fall of snow overnight, I went to the sets in an attempt to follow the activities of the badgers by their tracks in the snow. Frost of 19°F. still persisted at 8 o'clock, but the badgers had been in and out of the main and corner sets. They had also paid a visit to the unoccupied set at the west end. The fallen scratching tree across the bed of the pool had come in for attention, too, and was well trodden along its snow-covered length. They had been to the kale field feeding on the stems, and wandered slithering over the ice of the pond where their spoors were mingled with those of hungry rat and stoat.

I noticed that during the cold spell they had been pulling ivy from the big oak above the sand banks. I had not seen signs of their taking this before, and I think they were probably driven to it by shortage of more palatable food.

A rabbit shoot in the dell gave them a good feed. The rabbits were gutted on the spot and a considerable feast of offal lay in the bottom of the dell. It was not touched till the following night when I heard and saw badgers feeding on it in the moonlight. The noise with which they relished the feast could only be compared with those of a very ill-mannered old gentleman taking soup in great haste.

A break in the cold weather came after the first week in February, and the badgers were immediately busy spring cleaning the sets, with particular attention to those on the sand banks. The farmer was doing some clearing in preparation for the ploughing of the pasture. There was a general trimming-up round the boundaries of the dell, and all undergrowth was cleared from the field hedges.

The badgers were now deprived of practically all low cover, and this, with the rabbit and pigeon shooting during the daytime, may have accounted for the fact that they had become very furtive and difficult to watch. Another factor that contributed to this was the ploughing of the pasture. Four heavy tractors were employed and there was almost continuous daily work of ploughing, harrowing, sowing and rolling for some time. Fortunately, a small area of pasture bordering the north and east sides of the dell was left unploughed.

The weather was very poor throughout March with persistent cloud during what should have been a moonlit period. But clear nights came in April, and on the 11th, waiting by the sand banks, I heard cubs squealing and the familiar bubbling call of the sow. The sounds were of very short duration, and were listened to intently by a boar badger that came out from the set I was watching. They came from the north-east corner, and he stood out on the platform in front of the sandy set, his head turned in that direction while he appeared to be listening with interest.

My main concern was to see the new cubs at the earliest possible date, but I knew it was unlikely they would be above ground often in the cold nights we were having. But on the night of April 17 the thermometer rose sharply to 40°F. and after the emergence of a sow badger from the main set entrance, one small cub came out alone. It looked about seven weeks old, and climbed up from the set with difficulty on its yet wobbly legs. It was above ground for only a few minutes, then turned to tumble down the set nose first.

Needless to say, the next evening saw me posted as near as I could get, with safety, to the set entrance. Several badgers appeared early on the sand banks, then, to my exasperation, I heard the cubs and the answering sow at the north-east corner!

This brought certainty to something that had long been a suspicion in my mind. Since last autumn I had been puzzled by the frequent changing of sets on the part of the badgers. I could never tell whether they would emerge from the corner or the sandy set, and frequently found myself at the wrong one. As I have related, they appeared to spend no more than a day or two at either. The

79

entrances were about 130 feet apart, and it now seemed likely that there was an underground way connecting two or more sets between these openings. This was made more certain when the cubs appeared at the main set entrances a few days after they were heard at the north-east corner set. The possibility that the sow had moved the cubs from one set to another and back again could be discredited. The cubs were not yet sufficiently strong and active to make the journey above ground. There was no evidence that they were going farther than the immediate vicinity of the set; they were not using the latrine.

It was an exciting moment when, watching at the main set, on April 21, I saw two enquiring little faces appear in the entrance. The cubs hesitated and drew back. But in a short time they came right out, followed immediately by the sow and two more cubs. They did not go far from the set entrance, but busied themselves snuffing the ground over the platform outside. A delightful feature of their movements was the way in which they 'twinkled' their fluffy white tails. There was not much play. One attempt to bite the sow's nose drew a rebuff, and she playfully snapped at the cub. Once or twice two of the cubs faced up to one another as though to begin a romp. But these attempts at play did not go far, for the cubs were not yet strong on the legs, and it needed only a gentle push from one to send another rolling. They were out for half an hour that night, and were left alone by the sow for some time.

At this early age the cubs' appearances are not regular, and I did not see them next evening. But on the 23rd they came out, though later than before. The following night, in spite of a temperature of only 34°F. and a north wind, they were out at 9 o'clock. One cub was tucked underneath the sow as she emerged, and peeped out from between her front legs. This is probably a typical protective action, as something similar has been witnessed by Ernest Neal.

The cubs were now a little more playful and venturesome, one or two going as far as twelve feet from the set, but they were still unsteady on their legs. On level ground they were safe enough, but any uneven surface was liable to send them tottering. One, approaching the set from behind, fell head over heels into it, but seemed no worse for his adventure. They were very attractive at this early age, and I felt I now had great reward for past cold, cramp, and all other discomforts.

BADGER FAVOURS

THE COLD WEATHER CONTINUED WITH BITTER north-east winds. Though the adults were out every night, the cubs were emerging late or not at all. But a fine evening with moonlight followed several wet days, and the sow emerged with three cubs at 10 o'clock. They were now more active, running up and down the sand banks, their busy little noses exploring every inch of the way.

There was an ash tree about six feet from the set opening, one that I had always despised as being too small to hide the watcher, for there was no cover around the base. I noticed that the cubs were attracted to it, sniffing along the bare roots and into every little hollow. I was standing by a tree a yard or two away, and they soon came to my feet. They snuffed among the leaves and round my boots for several minutes, and I seemed to convey no sense of danger to them. I wondered how far their trust would go.

Next morning I poured syrup over the roots of the ash, and in the evening sat down to wait, hidden by the tree, with my legs covered by a light screen of foliage I had erected earlier in the day. I held a coconut shell full of honey against the roots where I hoped the cubs would come.

What I endured in cramp behind that tree I will not relate. My troubles were increased by the fact that I had only to lean a little to one side and I was sure to make a visible bulge beyond the trunk.

I spent an anxious few minutes when the sow first emerged and appeared to examine every aspect of her surroundings. But I was not seen. I heard the cubs come out from the lower opening, and wander away to the bottom of the dell. Several adults passed by without detecting me, but one coming up the bank opposite to my tree, stopped, stared, and fled the way she had come. She may have seen me, or merely been disturbed by the unusual shape of the low screen covering my legs, for badgers get used to the form of every bush or tree around the set, and any alteration in contour is quickly noticed.

I had not long to wait for the cubs. Three came to the near-by hazel and started to dig up and eat pignuts. They soon found the raisins I had thrown out, and these led them to the syrup. They could never have tasted it before but, to my delight, all three started to lap it at once.

The sow was near, and unfortunately rats scuffling in the dry leaves startled her. She ran for the set and the cubs followed, but they did not go in. The lure was too great, and in no time they were back, jostling one another to get at the syrup. I offered the honey to the nearest, and he lapped it for a moment, then turned again to the syrup on the root. I dipped my fingers in the honey and offered it again. The cub was too young to have much sense of danger, yet he must have had an inherited caution that told him to beware of the stranger. He nosed my fingers, and drew back a few inches as though a little suspicious. But that was his only reaction, and he went on lapping the syrup on the roots almost touching my hand. Not a drop of syrup was left on the tree when, at last, the cubs finished eating and went back to the set, to curl up replete on their warm, dry bed underground.

This was a beginning, and I felt that with care and patience the mistrust might be overcome. I hardly dared to hope for the night when a cub would take the syrup from my hand.

The next evening I waited again sitting by the ash, having laid syrup on the roots, and holding the coconut shell containing bread and syrup. Three cubs emerged at 9.40 and made at once for the tree. After lapping the syrup for a long time one turned to the coconut, but he seemed uncertain and went on lapping from the root. When most of the syrup had gone, they returned to the set and gave me the opportunity to put out some more. The cubs were soon back, romping this time with the sow. They came to the tree and began to take the syrup once more. They lapped fast and fur-iously, their little noses pressed hard against one another to get every drop. I offered my coconut, but again the cub only tasted the syrup and drew aside to lap from the tree. The gentle movement of my hand did not disturb the cubs, and I took out the bread hoping the syrup alone would be more acceptable. The nearest cub started to take it at once, but it was not long before his nose came up against my thumb. This made him withdrew a few inches, as though not quite sure of the strange contact.

The cubs stayed eating a long time, and I was able to see them very well in the moonlight. I had never thought to make such close contact with badgers in the wild, and my position on the ground brought me so near to them that I could see every detail.

It is difficult to describe the charm of badger cubs, particularly of those seen in the wild, for none born in captivity could have the clean and dapper appearance of these little creatures of the countryside. They were irresistible; perfect small editions of the adults except that their fur was more fluffy and a much lighter grey. I was fascinated by their dark ears edged with snow-white fur, and their fluffy, twinkling tails. The charm of the dark facial stripe running through the white head was very marked in the beautiful curves as the cubs turned their heads this way and that to lick the syrup. They were very expressive, and at times humorous, in their sudden movements and the way they pushed snub nose to snub nose along the tree roots to get the last of the syrup.

It was notable that the syrup seemed to have no attraction for the sow. It was an anxiety lest she should come to feed and discover me, for I knew that her reactions would be conveyed to the cubs and possibly instil them with a caution they now lacked. Yet on one occasion she came to sit down only a few feet from my hand, and I was not seen. I was frozen in a breathless tension till she wandered away leaving the cubs to their feast.

Unfortunately badger cubs are not the only creatures that find syrup irresistible. Several rats had bothered me one evening, and now they were becoming an intolerable nuisance. They persistently lapped the syrup from the tree before the badgers emerged, and my efforts to scare them off were not very effective because I was limited to actions that were silent and would not disturb the badgers.

One night when the sow and cubs emerged the rats made such a scuffling in the dry leaves that the whole family turned tail down the set. They were out again almost at once, but the continual rustling from the rats

around my tree deterred them from coming near, and soon cubs and adults all went down the bank out of sight and hearing.

I waited patiently in the hope that they would come back, and meanwhile the rats became more and more audacious. They would not be shooed away, and came right in under my hands to get at the raisins put out for the badgers. I lunged at them with a stick but they only came back for more. When I attacked from the front, they crept up on me from behind, or under my legs. And while I was shooing one, another would creep round the bole of the tree to lick the syrup almost off my hand. They were all sizes: huge rats, bigger than any I had seen before; old and mangy rats; rats in their prime; and little new rats of the spring; all ready to risk anything for a taste of the syrup.

The badgers were out of hearing, and at last, in desperation, I threw handfuls of soil, sticks, pebbles, anything handy, at the rats, but nothing deterred the brutes, and when I visited the tree next morning I found they had even been gnawing the roots to get the last drop of sweetness from them.

The next night I laid a syrup trail through the bushes to lure the rats away, and they were not as troublesome as they had been, but I did not put out enough to supply the hungry horde and they were soon back to bother me again. When I arrived on the following evening, the largest rat was sitting up on her hind legs waiting for me. She came up boldly to get the syrup before I finished laying the trail!

To my disappointment the badgers were now emerging much later, and seemed to have given up the paths along the top of the dell, and past the ash tree. They had formed a habit of taking the path leading down the bank. It may be that the bright moonlight made them seek the darker and shadowed ways.

The weather was poor, with strong north winds. I spent evenings in a tree that rocked like a ship on the ocean; I tried the precipice, taking my treacle with me, and standing for hours with the coconut shell in my hand, often in some twisted position, to reach a suitable place beside a badger path where I hoped the cubs would pass. It was impossible to avoid spilling the syrup over my clothes in the dark and unwittingly I turned myself into a Pied Piper, luring the rats to me everywhere I went. It was impossible to get away from them. If I stood up they climbed the bushes, and I felt them nosing my hand that held the sketch-book.

That week all my theories about badgers disliking wind and rough weather were quashed. On the evening of May 16, a very blustery night with cold, strong north winds and some rain, two adults and four cubs were out at 9.30, and played for a long time on the sand banks. The cubs were racing about in the bottom of the dell, their excited little yelps heard above the wind that set every tree creaking and groaning. They were just as happy on several nights following when I shivered in a cruel north-east wind that sent the thermometer down to freezing by the morning.

At this time I planned to intercept the cubs on the path leading down from the set to the foot of the dell. I cut out a hollow where I could sit on the steep bank beside the path, there some low bushes gave a little cover. The roots of the big oak proved to be a maze of rats' holes. If the rats were not climbing over my legs, they were

crawling round my shoulders, but they were not much trouble once the badgers were out, and it was here I had my greatest success with feeding the cubs. They would peep at me round the bush, and feed at once from the coconut full of syrup or a piece of wood dipped in it. One night a cub threatened to eat the entire stick as well. He tugged it almost out of my hand, and chewed the pieces he bit off with relish. I wondered whether so much wood with his treacle was going to agree with them, and exchanged it for the syrup-filled coconut. He lapped for a long time, and was in no way put off by the close contact of my fingers that held the rim.

When I was sitting at the foot of a hawthorn next night, I had the cubs gathered closely round me several times. They seemed now to accept me, and would stand a foot or so away regarding me without concern. They were very playful, and discovering an old, half-rotten log of wood, tried to tear it to pieces, clawing and biting at it with tremendous noise. This seemed to give them a taste for destruction, and one day, soon after, I found they had attacked the old tree that lay on its side below the sand banks. It was more or less hollow, and they had torn great lumps several times their own size from it, and must have found their way inside. I was not sorry, for one night a rat had climbed up my coat from that tree as I leaned against the trunk. It was a rats' stronghold.

They had another stronghold under the tree where I sometimes sat, east of the set, to feed the cubs. Late one night, when the rats had finished most of the food I had laid to lure them away, a number converged on me there. They came up on all sides. My fingers were snapped, and one great brute made continual rushes at my legs.

I knew that these delightful experiences of feeding the cubs could not go on indefinitely, and after a while the syrup

86

failed to have the overwhelming attraction for them. One night they spent a long time around the main set, stretching on the hazel stem outside the entrance, and coming and going around the ash tree close to the syrup, yet they passed it. On another occasion they galloped over my outstretched hand holding the sugared stick, ignoring it and me.

I think this gradual indifference to the syrup may have been caused by weaning, and the change over to more substantial diet. It is said that even adult badgers find syrup irresistible, but these observations have been derived from animals in captivity. It is true that they delight in a feed of wasps' or bees' nest, but it may be largely the grubs among the honey that contribute to the tastiness of the meal. What a badger will eat in captivity is a very unreliable indication of his diet in the wild. I know of one instance where a captive badger was fed largely on eggs, which it relished, and this incident sadly maligned the badgers' character in that district, the landowners getting the erroneous impression that they spend most of their nights at nesting time looking for pheasants' eggs.

My chances of continuing to feed the cubs were jeopardised by a spell of wet and windy weather. Also the badgers were going through one of their quiet periods. The cubs were not emerging till about 10.30. Wind direction was a great handicap, severely limiting my choice of positions where I might hope to intercept the cubs.

Ten days of June had now passed, and there was a sudden return to activity on the part of the badgers, but they were not living up to their reputation of emerging earlier in this month. By June 16 they had changed over to the north-east entrance, and this gave me a chance to see them in better light, though the wind drove me to sitting in a bed of nettles where I was attacked by swarms of mosquitoes!

In a week the badgers were emerging from the main set once more, and I returned to the ash tree. Sometimes they came and sniffed the syrup but, to my disappointment, failed to take it. One of last year's cubs came near to sampling it from the coconut shell I was holding, but as I expected, she had acquired something of the adults' wariness, and looking up at me, hesitated and drew back. I was glad to see that she made no frightened rush to the set, but merely walked away.

It is difficult to look at badger cubs without recalling the panda, and one night I wondered what they would do with the panda's

favourite food of bamboo shoots. I took some from the garden and left them near the set. That night one cub sat for a time nibbling them, but they were ignored by the rest of the family.

It had always been my ambition to see a badger take a bath, but my encouragement in that direction met with no success. At great labour I took a dustbin lid and water to the dell one morning, sunk the lid, and two nights later waited hopefully to see what the badgers would do with an improvised bathroom. The cubs came no further than contemplating it while I was there. I found their claw marks in the soil round it next day, yet it proved to serve only as a bird bath.

On midsummer night the badgers put on a delightful performance, coming out in good light and playing round the main set entrance for a long time. The two generations of cubs were at play together, and they harassed the patient sow while she struggled to groom herself amidst the mêlée. At length they dispersed, and after a long wait I decided to go home, for I had heard the family go away towards the pasture and knew that it might be some hours before they returned.

On my way back across the fields, I found myself suddenly surrounded by badgers. They were sweeping through the long, dew-laden grass, and I could see the little grey shapes of the cubs as they came repeatedly round me and up the bank to a big elm on the ridge. I stood still, wishing I might eat some of Alice in Wonderland's magic mushroom, and bring myself down to reasonable height, for I feared that my dark and sinister shape would be seen by the badgers with dire results. But their vision was limited by the tall grass, and under cover of the continual rustling, I made my way to the foot of the elm. Here the ground was bare for an area round the base of the tree, and every now and then the cubs would rustle out of the surrounding grass to circle the tree, almost brushing my feet.

At last they drifted away, and I stood alone in the starlit silence. Perhaps the summer midnight had worked its charm on me, or it may be that badger-watchers, in company with bird-watchers, are not entirely human. I felt I had encountered a moment of rare good fortune, and that here, in company with those merry wanderers, I had met the fabulous spirit of mid-summer night.

EARLY RISING

ONE NIGHT TOWARDS THE END OF JUNE THE badgers made a combined effort to bring in bedding from the pasture which had now been cut. The light was good, and I followed, making my way out of the spinney to walk slowly along the hedge bordering the field.

Several adults were pulling grass while the cubs alternated their attempts to practise the art with wild rushes and scampers about the field. They made so much noise that I was able to walk right up to the badgers without being discovered. I stood for a long time watching the busy scene, being sheltered by the dark background of the hedge behind me, and a small patch of nettles at my feet. When at last I left, the cubs ran along beside me either oblivious or carefree of my presence.

The grass was to the badgers as a candle to a moth, and next morning I found the entrances to the set piled high, as though the family effort had brought in so much bedding that the underground chambers were filled to overflowing.

On June 30 the badgers emerged early for the first time this year. They came out at 9.30, and the cubs raced round the dell in full daylight having suddenly become very bold. On another evening I was surprised to see one of last year's cubs emerge and go away at 9.5. There was no hesitation, and she seemed to have little sense of fear. After this she frequently came out at 9 o'clock, and one night was away by 8.33. She was often accompanied by one of this season's cubs that seemed equally bold. They made an amusing couple, usually emerging covered with sand, to trot away as though on important business. From my position by the set I was

within eight feet of the emerging badgers, though I was never discovered and had good opportunities for sketching.

One night I witnessed a little domestic scene in which the boar took an unusual part. A cub, having come down the slope from the main opening above, was met by him in a nose to nose greeting, then, to my surprise, he was rolled over and groomed by the boar. This serves to show that badger fathers are not above lending a hand——or should I say tongue?——in family affairs.

Badgers make good-tempered parents. The cubs would climb over the sow continually while she was trying to groom herself. They played hide-and-seek round her, clawed her in an attempt to make her join in their play, and generally tormented her, yet she was never irritable with them. The boar was subjected to similar treatment. The cubs climbed on him, played leap-frog over him, and raced round and round harrying him in a way that would have tried the patience of any human father, yet he remained good-tempered, and between his grooming joined in the play.

The cubs of last year continued to live with the family, and I was able to make a count of nine badgers emerging from the sand banks on July 5. One of the mature cubs came out first, followed by the boar and four cubs. The sow was the next to appear, and after her, two more adults. These were two of last year's offspring.

Unfortunately the cornfield was becoming more and more attractive to the badgers with the result that they would often emerge to go immediately to the field though they had to run the gauntlet in daylight to get there. Once in the corn they would usually be away for an indefinite period. I would follow to the edge of the field where I had to be content with no more than the occasional call of the cubs at play that came to me from a distance. Silence often followed, and I felt they had travelled well out of hearing, perhaps not to return till morning.

But later it became their habit to forage near the edge of the field. I had noticed the entire absence of rats in the dell during the last few weeks, for they were out making inroads on the corn. Listening on a still night I could sometimes hear their frantic squeals followed by the sounds of a badger enjoying a succulent meal, and I wished this good work might be as evident to the farmer as the paths the badgers made by their wanderings through the corn.

One night I attempted to delay them by scattering raw meat. The first out was a cub of last season. She stopped dead in her tracks when she scented the meat on the path. Sniffing it, she looked up accusingly in my direction, stepped carefully round the titbit, and went on. Torrential rain then spoilt any chance of seeing other badgers' reactions.

The field became a habit, but one evening with a change of wind from south to north, they took the path leading down to the foot of the dell. It seems not to be an infallible rule, but I have often noticed that badgers favour going into the wind when leaving a set. I have watched them scenting up-wind only, as though they appreciated the poor chance of scenting anything down-wind.

My greatest surprise came in daylight in this same year. I had gone to the dell to make sketches of the sets. It was my habit to approach quietly, but on this particular morning I took no special care in that respect, for I had been to the sets countless times in daylight without seeing badgers above ground. I walked along the bank beside the opening to the west set which to my knowledge had not been in use since last summer. I had just passed it when, hearing a rustle, I glanced aside to see a badger making its way along the path at the edge of the dell. It was about fifteen feet away, and passed from my view beyond some bushes. I hastily stepped behind the nearest cover, a diminutive hawthorn that boasted no more than a single stem. A further rustling in the undergrowth indicated the badger's direction, and almost at once two badgers came into view: the dark-tailed sow and a cub. They passed within eight feet of where I stood, the brilliant sunlight dappling their coats as they trotted unconcernedly to the set and went in.

I never expected to see badgers returning home at 10 a.m. No doubt they had been in the cornfields, and may have fallen asleep there in the early hours, or travelled too far on their night's wanderings. I crept silently into the thick cover of a tree stub wondering if they might come out again to join the rest of the family in the sand banks. I put in a long wait, but once in the sanctuary of the west set they remained.

It would be interesting to see what time they would emerge that evening, and I watched the set, arriving early. They came out at 9.40 in spite of their late return. The sow's first action was to get some bedding, as though this long deserted set lacked the amenity of a comfortable bed. Having brought in two bundles she retired

with the cub for rest, but in a quarter of an hour she came out to get more bedding. The cub ran back and forth with her, and was very playful, his exuberance carrying him, at times, up and down the bole of a big oak near-by. Meanwhile the sow, anxious to get her bedding into the set by the shortest route, was approaching the entrance from the back. The cub watched with interest as she fell in with a resounding thump, to grab her bundle at the last minute before she disappeared from view.

After a few nights at this set the sow and cub rejoined the family. Early emergence continued, and the badgers were all living together again. Last year's cubs were often seen in company with the offspring of this season. But on July 26 a great clearance of the set began, and the cubs were banished to the north-east corner. They emerged from there on several successive nights, with the exception of one cub that came out from the main set at 8.30 on the night of July 28.

Great quantities of sand and chalk were being turned out from the main and lower openings in the sand banks. One of last year's cubs was doing most of the work. She would emerge to begin almost at once. Standing close to the set I watched her many times as she came out backwards, dragging her load in much the same way as she would take a bundle of bedding. She brought it to the edge of the platform, then with vigorous kicks of the hind legs sent it flying to the depths below. There was a fearsome clatter as it hurtled to the bottom of the dell, and on each occasion she would glance over her shoulder as though startled by her own efforts. No doubt it was hard work, for the sand and chalk had to be brought from a distance underground. Time after time she came out with her load, panting under the effort.

Badgers enjoy rolling, and it was delightful to see how this cub of last year would, in the middle of a mock battle, roll over and let the attacking cubs bite and torment her at will. A badger on its back presents a picture of carefree bliss; a state of perfect contentment. I have seen cubs lie for some time showing their fluffy, light undersides; black legs pointing skywards, completely oblivious of my close company.

The clearance of the set in the sand banks continued, and one night it seemed that all this display of energy was being emulated by the cubs. They gave an amusing performance, scratching up with their front feet and kicking out with their back, in similar actions to those of the badger that had been clearing the set.

One cub in particular seemed delighted with the new antics, and stayed behind to play the game alone for some time after the others had gone to the field. She was a comic little figure, repeating again and again the sequence of actions in very quick time. It was all done where the soil was too hard to be scratched up, yet she persisted, snuffing the ground before each effort, and kicking out her back legs with such vigour that she was frequently off the ground, all four feet at once. At last, bubbling over with fun, she raced after the other cubs.

The badgers had remained unmolested since the gassing in the early part of last year, and it was a joy to see the spirit of happiness that prevailed in the colony. Watching this whole-hearted expression of life it seemed incredible that anyone should wish to destroy it.

I enlisted help that the two sets might be watched, but the deadly gas forestalled me. The west set was shallow, and any badgers there at the time had no chance of escape. From this time all early emergence ceased. I never saw last year's adventurous cub again, or counted more than seven badgers. They would slip quietly away to the fields, and I watched them with misgiving. I realized I had become too interested in this family which I had thought could be watched impartially.

During the daylight observations I had been able to identify the different badgers clearly. Tails were a good mark of recognition. The boar's tail was narrow and finely pointed; the sow's, even in poor light, appeared darker than any other; while the cubs all had conspicuous, fluffy white tails. The daring offspring of last year had a long, wispy paint brush which trailed the ground; it was stained golden with the sand. The cub that was often seen out early with her boasted a particularly fine, rounded tail like a big, fluffy powder-puff.

BOAR   LAST YEAR'S ADVENTUROUS CUB   DARK TAILED SOW   POWDER PUFF

It was also possible to identify some of the badgers by their behaviour on emerging. This was very marked in the sow and boar. Usually out early, the boar was slow and deliberate in his movements. He would raise and lower his head, peering into the bushes, scenting the air. Satisfied that nothing was amiss, he would enjoy his scratch, or wander away to the field as the spirit moved him. But the sow would wait for dusk to fall before making her appearance. She was furtive, running from side to side of the platform, scenting repeatedly before attempting a rush to the fields.

Probably the happiest part of any badger's life is spent in the early hours of the day when the chance of contact with man is very remote. There appears then to be a complete abandonment of discretion, and any watching done in those hours well repays the early riser. It certainly needs enthusiasm to get up from one's bed long before dawn, but there is a feeling of great triumph in being out along the lanes while behind curtained windows fellow beings snore on oblivious of all the sense of mystery and wonder one feels in the countryside at this hour. But there are many difficulties for the watcher; few sets offer conditions favourable to a silent approach. I was fortunate in this respect in the dell for I was able to keep a path clear through the bushes, and approaching over pasture sometimes walked within a few feet of badgers, themselves rustling the ground cover on the edge of the field, and so unsuspecting, that I passed without suspicion.

Badgers are very expressive, both in action and voice. There is no doubt that to hear them to the best advantage the watcher should be up early. Going to the dell before dawn one day in August, I heard them at a distance of 300 yards across the fields. They were all giving voice at once, and young cries were mingled with adult rumbles and yelps of such high spirits it seemed the badgers had not a care in the world.

I knew myself for an intruder as I slipped unseen into the shelter of the tree east of the main set. A badger lingered for some minutes on the bank, seeming reluctant to take her last look at the waking world, while behind her the cubs, still noisily protesting, trotted away into the supposed security of the set.

It was marvellous to see how the badgers' simple environment could give so much pleasure. The playing tree near the set was one of their greatest entertainments. The cubs would race round and round and up and over it; play king-of-the-castle on the base; or stay to stretch their young limbs and claws on the sloping branches. It was also a natural drinking fountain, and between play little tongues would lap noisily at the rain pools in its gnarled hollows.

I have seen the cubs playing on this tree in the evening, and by the light of the same moon watched them there again at 3.30 a.m. eclipsing their play of the night before. Coming in wet from the field they shook their coats vigorously before a riot of play with mock fighting in which several rolled together, a squealing ball of fur, at my feet. Wild rushes and scuffles took them away round the bushes to trace back again, panting with their exertions. In the midst of all this they broke off suddenly and turned to the playing tree, one taking possession on its base, and the others trying by every means to dislodge him. It was difficult not to laugh outright when one grabbed another by the tail and pulled him from the tree.

Adults and cubs drifted back to the set singly and in pairs. The last was home by 5 o'clock. The full moon was going down over the cornfields as dawn broke beyond the farm now coming to life with the lowing of cows. I looked regretfully behind me at the sleeping dell, and wandered home across the fields hardly knowing to which world I belonged.

FINDINGS FOR THE YEAR 1954

Three of the previous year's cubs were still seen to be with the parents in January.

Four cubs were born to the original pair in February, and first heard to emerge on April 11. One was seen above ground on the night of April 17, and the family of four were first seen on April 21.

At this time, last year's cubs were emerging from the north-east corner, and were living apart from the parents and the new cubs. They returned to live with the family in the sand banks at the beginning of June, and remained there till the end of July when two were thought to be occupying the west set where they succumbed to gassing. The third continued to live in the family set.

Through October and November there were temporary divisions of the family when for no more than a few days at a time some of the badgers left the sand banks to take up residence at the north-east corner set. It was during one of these divisions that all the sets were gassed, and re-gassed.

ANOTHER TRAGEDY

DURING THE WINTER AND THE EARLY PART of 1955 I did some watching with the aid of a torch. I had great success, for though the badgers had been made very timid by the gassing, in time they regained their confidence and were remarkably indifferent to the light. They would come up to my feet with the torch still directed on them, and it was rare for one to do more than draw back a little on contact.

The peanuts I had been putting out during the cold weather were still a great attraction in March, and the badgers would come up from the sand banks regularly every night to search for nuts in accustomed places. They took them from round my feet, and would follow the track of my steps nose-down till they arrived at the food. One night an early riser cleared the board, and before I could put out any more nuts a second badger came out to look for her share. Finding none in the expected places, she began to follow my steps. She snuffed the ground anxiously, hurrying in frantic haste round the bushes where I had walked. Finally, after a fruitless search she arrived at my feet. She looked up reproachfully and wandered away.

There was no doubt that my scent was connected with the sought-after delicacy of peanuts, and I wondered if it would be possible to feed an adult badger by hand, as I fed the cubs last spring. I had little hope of success, but next evening I sat on the ground by a tree to offer a coconut-shell full of peanuts and raisins. I had laid a short trail of nuts, and this brought the first badger out, to within a few inches of my hand. She drew back, but I felt she might be persuaded.

The following night I tried again. I had scarcely any cover in the bright moonlight, and only the few twigs I had put up prevented the badger from getting an unimpeded view of my figure as I sat on the bank. She ate the few nuts I had scattered, then sat looking at the tempting affluence held out to her. She crept forward and touched the coconut-shell with her nose and leapt back at once to sit regarding it, then, to my disappointment, turned away. But the nuts were still on her mind, and after snuffing the ground in vain on a journey in my footsteps, she came back. This time she snatched a nut from under the rim of the shell. It was hastily gobbled, and another snatched. She came forward again, her head stretched out to the nuts. I waited breathlessly. She thrust her nose into the shell, took out a nut and sat back to eat it. Several more were taken in this way, then finding nothing untoward had happened to her, she came and sat down to enjoy the feast. She was now confident, and the close proximity and the scent of my hand did not trouble her. She repeatedly pushed my thumb up with her nose to get at the nuts underneath, and I could not resist the temptation to rub her nose in return, a liberty to which she took no exception.

Determined to get every nut, her long and useful claws were brought into action to retrieve the most elusive, and as a final show of familiarity, she came round to take a last peanut almost from under my sleeve.

She strolled back to the set with an air of great satisfaction. I wondered if her evening could have been as rewarding as my own.

On April 8, Good Friday, all the sets were gassed again.

Some badgers made their way out, and I continued to watch. Observation was difficult with the badgers emerging late and very furtive owing to the disturbance of gassing which continued almost weekly throughout April and May.

I watched persistently but it was not till May 23, that I saw cubs. Two emerged from the main set, but they were very backward in their behaviour, and ventured only a few yards from the set openings.

The sets had been stopped so many times that the badgers now had difficulty in making fresh entrances. They had come out to one side of the original opening, and the way up was so steep that the cubs seemed to have a struggle to climb out. On several nights following their first appearance I heard them whimpering in the set for a long time before emergence. But after about a week the sets were gassed again, and the second family appeared with the first, making four cubs and four adults in all. The cubs were now much more active, but on May 31, I saw them at play for the last time. No badgers survived a final gassing on June 1.

THE PIGGERY SET

IWAS ALMOST DETERRED BY THE HUGE BOAR PIG and his nine wives whose territory surrounded the badgers' sets I proposed to watch. My doubts were greeted with the usual assurance, "He won't hurt, not that old boar. He's a quiet one."

In my experience most farm animals are given these mild credentials, but I know of at least one 'quiet old bull' which sent a badger watcher fleeing for life through a prickly hedge in the dark. I cast a doubtful eye on the torn, solitary glove that lay inside the piggery, for it suggested a more than hasty retreat on the part of its owner. I was not without trepidation as I climbed over the wire into the piggery for the first time.

The badgers had excavated their sets on level ground above a small chalk-pit full of old elder bushes; an unusual choice where so much sloping ground was available. A vast amount of chalk had been turned out from the two main openings of one of the sets, and within an area of about thirty feet by fifty I found no fewer than twelve entrances. Only one had been made in the bank of the pit. The whole area was heavily trampled by pigs, and in one place they had gone through into the badgers' tunnel, making an entrance that was not intended. The large number of holes, and the fact that many were often in use, made watching very difficult, as it was almost impossible to find a position where scent would not be carried to one or more of the holes, though the wind might be favourable to others.

Apart from this difficulty it was not easy to find a position where one could hope to remain unseen. The pigs had eaten every vestige of ground cover over the area. Anyone sheltering behind the few scattered hawthorns in front of the sets would be seen against the sky by the emerging badgers. This is always a bad position for the watcher, as badgers are familiar with the shapes of trees and bushes round their sets and will easily detect any change. The only hawthorn which would have given fair cover was in use by the badgers as a playing tree.

Behind the sets there was a dense planting of hawthorns, but I was not keen to entangle myself in there with the pigs, whose sleeping huts would have been only a short distance behind me. Apart from this, the area was a maze of badger paths, and the chances of being discovered were great.

All the bushes had been stripped of foliage by the pigs just below eye level, and I was forced either to stand with bent back to peer under the boughs, a position which became unbearable in a very short time, or to sit on the ground where there was no cover. I rarely find a sitting position favourable, as the range of vision becomes very limited from the low level, and one's limbs are quickly cramped. There is another disadvantage in the fact that it is almost impossible to get up without making some disturbance, and as I like, sometimes, to be ready to follow the badgers on their wanderings, I prefer to stand.

Altogether, watching prospects in the piggery were not promising. But occupied sets in the district were rare. Most of the badgers had been killed by gassing, which had been intensified in the hysterical panic among landowners, which followed the passing of the rabbit through myxomatosis. The fear that badgers would turn to killing poultry and game in lieu of rabbits sounded the knell for many innocent badgers. I found colony after colony destroyed.

I had experienced so much of the results of cruelty and ignorance, it was a pleasure to be able to watch sets that were not molested. The owner of the land containing these sets appreciated the animals' worth, and was of the opinion that wild life should not be destroyed merely because it might, at some time, cause slight inconvenience to mankind. Foxes, too, were undisturbed, and played their part in keeping down harmful rodents.

My first evening in the piggery was encouraging. I had been waiting only a few minutes when a badger cub looked out from a set entrance in daylight on one side, while on the other, appeared the elfin figure of a fox cub. He had squeezed under the wire from a second dell that bordered the piggery, and stood on the bank a

short distance away. He stared in my direction, eyes intensely awake, his furry ears pricked, his small, dark nose scenting the air expectantly.

It was not possible to make a full count of the badgers on the first evening, as my position could not command unrestricted views of all the set entrances that may have been in use. A sow came out soon after the first cub had been seen at the entrance. With her were two cubs and a boar whose distinctive appearance would make him easily recognisable in future, for he had more white on the head and neck than I had previously seen on any badger.

There was soon a joyous exhibition of play, including leap-frog, and climbing on the trunk of a hawthorn near the set. Other badgers were seen and heard. They had, presumably, come from entrances hidden from view.

The pigs were more or less asleep that night, but arriving early next evening I was confronted by a sow which was still ranging. She stood by, watching my efforts to cut and erect, as silently as possible, some small branches of hawthorn to form cover round the base of the bush where I proposed to stand. When it was arranged to my satisfaction, I retired to fetch the binoculars I had left hanging on the fence. I returned in time to see the last remnants of my hide disappearing into the mouth of the sow, whose wrinkled face wore the traces of a satisfied smile!

I realised that any foliage erected within reach of the pigs was useless, and my only hope lay in collecting dead wood to pile against the bushes. This should at least remain till one of the pigs chose to rub her back against my bush, and knock the hide down. Any cover should, of course, be erected during the day, and it may be, that for all my care, the badgers heard my movements.

It was surprising that the colony remained in the piggery, for the continual tramping of the pigs over the sets during the day must have been very disturbing for animals which took their sleep in the daylight hours. They could have used other near-by sets in more suitable situations, and I was disappointed to find they had left the sets in the foxes' dell which they used in the previous season. This dell was a perfect haven, so thickly overgrown with elders and clematis that none of the ground below could be seen from the top of the bank. The dell and the area of scrub beyond made a green, undulating vista of many acres, and I often wondered what secrets it held at night. I wished I could share the view with the innumerable pigeons which roosted there, and kept up a continuous cooing from sunset till dusk; a background to the songs of many woodland birds.

HARVESTING

JULY WATCHING GAVE POOR RESULTS. HAY-MAKING was in full swing, and the road that bordered the piggery was in constant use by tractors taking loads to the farm. After emergence, the badgers would sit close to the set entrances, and listen to the approaching traffic. As it turned the corner, about seventy yards away, they would scramble down the sets. Emergence was often disturbed in this way, and sometimes I waited till very late without seeing the badgers at all.

But in time they became almost indifferent to the traffic. If they were outside the set entrance when a tractor passed, they might return slowly to the set, but would usually sit watching till it had gone by.

The dry weather and resulting hard ground gave no indication of spoor, and it was difficult to know from which holes the badgers might emerge. One evening in July the cubs chose to come from an opening which I had not seen used for months. Because of the difficulties of wind direction, I was obliged to stand near this entrance, which was beside the subsidence hole made by the pigs. One hole was not more than four feet from my sheltering hawthorn. As I stood watching for badgers to emerge from the main opening, I heard 'talking' in the set near-by. Turning my head very slowly, I saw three cubs looking out from the hole beside me. I must have been very obvious in full daylight, and the cubs were not satisfied that this strange, new shape could be trusted. But they were anxious to come out and play. I watched two, and sometimes three enquiring little faces that appeared and disappeared frequently at the entrance. At last the most daring of the cubs came out, and went down a farther hole, but suspicion was too strong and the cubs did not appear again, though the adults left the set from the main entrance later.

Haymaking was followed by harvesting. Often as many as five tractors passed the piggery in the vital half hour in which I expected emergence, and on many watches no badgers were seen, though I stayed late at the sets. Yet during the week-end watching, when the harvesters were not working, there was little more activity.

The badgers were certainly active at some time during the night, for daylight showed a clearly marked path leading away through the foxes' dell. I followed it to a playground on the edge of the wood about two hundred yards from the sets. There was also a worn area round a playing tree and a set newly turned out. Well-trodden paths led away under the trees and bushes, and it seemed likely that the lack of badgers emerging in the piggery might be accounted for by some of their number having transferred their quarters to this set. But watches there proved fruitless.

The possibility that some of the badgers had gone elsewhere still existed, and I examined the sets on the bank across the pasture on the north. One out in the field had claw marks up the slope of the entrance, and appeared to be in use. I spent a long and uncomfortable wait there next night, lying among grass and thistles; the only cover. I waited in vain. Further searching by day showed no other sets which might be in use, and I came to the conclusion that the badgers' rare appearances supported my theory that they lay up considerably during periods of drought.

On August 12 there were a few showers of rain, and a resulting difference in behaviour that night. The first badger emerged at 9.23 B.S.T., and went away to forage immediately. A cub came out from another entrance at 9.30, and I was lucky not to be detected, as I was standing only about eight feet away. Another cub soon followed, and two more adults emerged later.

The next day was blessed with heavy rain all the afternoon. It slackened to a drizzle in the evening, and, as I expected, the badgers emerged earlier. The cubs could be heard at the main opening at 8.40, and four were soon out and at play. They raced away across the dell, and were followed by the boar. All had left the set by 9 o'clock.

The return to earlier emergence and general activity continued. The cubs were playful again, and they seemed to have become used to the harvesting activity. One night I saw two cubs and the boar emerge and stay to watch a very noisy tractor pass along the farm

road at a distance of about fifty yards. This was at 9 p.m., and all three badgers were away to their feeding grounds by 9.15. The fourth cub and the sow came out soon after. The cub spent some time turning out the set, and it was notable that most of the entrances showed signs of having been cleared since the rainfall.

I found that many of the entrances had been cleared again the following evening. The boar and sow emerged at 9.30, and soon three cubs came scrambling out to join them. They trotted away with the sow, towards the pasture on the other side of the farm road, and I could not attempt to follow as the boar remained, going in and out of the set, in very furtive mood. It was a long time before he went away.

He often made himself a nuisance, for he seemed to have a suspicious nature. He would look out of the main set, retire, and presently appear at another entrance from where he peered long and enquiringly in my direction, then returned into the set again to reappear at another hold. From every entrance where he looked out, his head was turned towards the watcher. Doubtless he had his suspicions of my presence, for it was very difficult to hide in the scant cover, though I did what I could from time to time by putting up brushwood against the hawthorns. These were unfortunately placed, as any cover erected round one position blocked the view of the sets from another. With twelve holes surrounding any stand, it was impossible to keep an eye on all, and I often felt the want of an elaborate system of mirrors. It would have been an advantage to block some of the holes; a few sticks in the openings would have put the badgers off using them, but I was reluctant to interfere with their natural use of the sets.

Towards the first week in September, there was another period of inactivity during the dry weather, and I found that the cubs had gone to a set on the steep, pasture bank. They were even more difficult to watch there. The set was at the top of the bank, and was thickly overhung with bushes. I cleared away some of the smaller branches, and made a watching position, without too much disturbance. But it could only be used when the wind was favourable, and difficulties were increased by the fact that the dung pits were at the foot of the bank, below the watcher, and a wind right for watching the set betrayed one's presence to any badger using the latrine.

Emerging badgers soon disappeared behind the bushes, and often went out at the top of the bank to the pasture where they were, at once, lost to view. Alternatively, they went to the cornfield below. There, if the watcher could be concealed in the bushes, the

badgers were seen clearly, for the corn had been harvested, and the stubble gave them no cover. But for the watcher in this position, the sets on the bank were obscured, and if the badgers took the other route after emergence, they were not seen at all.

A freshly turned-out set on the bank farther along suggested occupation, and the possibility that the parents had come across from the piggery. But a cleared set is not necessarily used, and I found that the set was only visited by the cubs resident in the steep part of the bank.

By September 19 they were back with the parents in the piggery where I saw four cubs and two adults out at 7.43 G.M.T. On September 23 I saw seven badgers emerge from this set. The next night wind direction took my scent to badgers which, unexpectedly, used a long-deserted path behind me. But the following evening I was able to count seven badgers again: two adults went away from the set first, and were soon followed by a sow and four cubs. But after this there was so much leaving and returning to the sets by various holes, that it became impossible to tell whether there were even more badgers now in residence. From my own and other naturalists' experience a rise in adult population at a set is often seen at this time of year, and is due to mating activity.

MOONLIGHT

OONLIGHT IS ALWAYS A TEMPTATION. It lures the watcher out hopefully, yet knowing that the badgers will be reluctant to show themselves in the light conditions. But such nights always reward the watcher with the beauty of the scene, which may be enhanced by the nightingale's song, or the mystic call of the plover in nuptial flight. There is also the fascination of listening for, and striving to see, the flocks of migrating birds that pass, ghost-like, across the moonlit sky.

Enjoyment is found in watching the variation of scene in the changes of light and shade. I used to watch a badgers' set at the top of a high, chalk slope where the formation of shadows had a unique beauty. A young ash tree grew half-way down the slope, and I often watched its shadow creep over the bank on moonlit nights. Arriving before dusk, I saw the shadow take form. At first it appeared as no more than a faint pencilling on the white slope. As the night darkened, the contrasts gradually brought the shadow into relief, defining the delicate form of foliage and boughs, perhaps more beautiful than the tree itself.

The same fascination is experienced in watching the shadows give way to daylight in the early hours. One morning in particular I remember vividly. I had gone to some badgers' sets, getting up from bed at 2.30 a.m. I arrived when the shadows were still densely black in contrast to the rest of the countryside which was shimmering with dew under the brilliance of a full moon.

I admit that my appreciation of the scene was slightly tempered by apprehension as I passed some of the darkest shadows, and I was not comforted when a loud cough suddenly broke the silence from a hollow in the field. Whether it was animal or human I could not tell. No cows had been in the pasture the previous evening, and the possibility that some vagrant or gipsy might be abroad on nefarious business came to mind. But I was in no mood for retreat after the effort of rising so early. I walked on and crept furtively into the woodland area that contained the badgers' sets.

The badgers returned, shook the dew from their coats, and raced helter-skelter round the bushes in high spirits, for no human form was likely to be encountered at this time in the morning. The world seemed all their own. After a while they retired down the set, and I was left in contemplation of the shadows. As I listened to the absolute silence, I heard a faint hush creep over the fields, a sound that was hardly perceptible, yet defining the change from night to day. With it, a white mist enveloped the countryside, and I watched the shadows gradually fade. The moon, which a few moments before had been almost dazzling in its brilliance, became a dull amber sphere through the thickening curtain of mist. The dawn broke.

The hours before sunrise are the best in which to see badgers. The absence of man's activity gives their enjoyment free rein, and all caution seems to be abandoned, as in this instance when, earlier in the night, the brilliant moonlight would have subdued the animals. The badgers in the piggery came out more freely as the moon waned, and on October 8 the cubs were all away by 6.45 p.m. and were soon followed by the sow and boar. There was no hope of seeing them back at the set for many hours. They had gone towards the bluebell wood which was bordered on the far side by stubble and clover fields, and I decided to try to follow, going round the wood in the opposite direction.

The difficulties of this kind of watching are great, but the noise of the energetic badgers foraging through the wood served me well. I reached the fields on the other side without alerting them, and was able to see them in the light of a torch as they climbed on the base of a leaning tree, and foraged through the undergrowth. I followed to the farm road where they usually crossed to the opposite pasture, and arrived in time to see the last badger's backward glance as they all scampered away down the valley.

The cubs were now nearly full grown, and it was often difficult to distinguish them from the adults in the rough and tumble of play which preceded their leaving the sets.

At this time of year, grooming is a marked feature of the badgers' behaviour. They frequently sit outside the sets after emergence nibbling each other's fur; a pastime they seem to enjoy. Several will sit close together facing in alternate directions, while they nibble one another's backs, heads, necks and ears. This becomes almost an evening habit, with all the badgers from a set taking part. Whether it has anything to do with mating activity it is difficult to say.

On the night of October 22, there was a lot of play among the seven badgers which emerged. There were several attempts at mating, and in the light of later developments it seemed probable that this was due to the arrival of newcomers which had joined the colony recently. Towards the end of October, the moon's first quarter was giving a good light, and the animals seemed reluctant to leave the proximity of the sets. There was an air of lethargy about the proceedings. The badgers would come out and sit by the entrances grooming one another for a while, before strolling in again, and on more than one occasion I watched the original boar make a leisurely emergence to sit above the set opening, yawning frequently, in a mood that might be translated in human terms as one of extreme boredom.

The weather was very cold with temperatures below freezing-point, and on some nights the drawn-out nature of emergence became trying for the watcher. The badgers appeared, and disappeared into the sets again over such a long period that it was almost a relief when the last had gone away, for by this time I was shivering with cold. The best of the year's watching was over.

Yet for all the disappointments there is a fascination in trying to see something of the badger's life through the winter months, and it is impossible to resist any night that offers an opportunity. November 5 was a fine night, and in spite of the prospect of Guy Fawkes activities, I was not discouraged, for I have seen badgers leave their sets and not make the expected return when fireworks were set off a few miles away. I hoped the badgers in the piggery would be equally indifferent. But it seemed that this November 5 was to be celebrated with a special flourish. I had never seen or heard such an extravagant display from any country district.

The boar came out from an entrance at the top of the bank at 5.50 p.m., but he was met with such a volley of noise and flashing lights that he retired hastily. At 6.5 two cubs and the sow ventured out of the same hole. One cub reached the playing tree and attempted to stretch his length against the trunk, and there was some play at the set entrance, for they all seemed eager to come out. But they were suddenly alarmed by a burst of fireworks, and rushed pell-mell down the set. Two made an attempt to emerge again at 7 o'clock, but they were obviously very upset by the noise and flickering lights which were, by then, floodlighting the sets. The badgers looked round, scenting the air in bewilderment, and staring furtively at the sudden explosive whoops and bangs that were now so concentrated there was no pause between. They quickly returned down the set and were not seen up to the time when I left, feeling they were not likely to come out again that night.

There was a lot of clearing of sets during the middle of November. Chalk was turned out in quantity with discarded bedding, and fresh grass bedding taken into the sets from the flat area above the foxes' dell. Even the sets in the steep bank across the pasture received this clearing in preparation for winter.

Other sets that I visited some miles away showed the same signs of activity, which is general at this time of year. I am convinced that where bedding is easily available badgers will bring it in much more frequently. The badgers in the piggery had to bring theirs from some distance, and I saw little brought in there, whereas I have often watched large quantities collected at other sets. To one set in a chalk bank, so much sere grass was brought from the wood above, that the badgers' path to the set had become paved with a thick, soft layer of bedding as though it had been used for the purpose frequently throughout many years.

WINTER AND BEYOND

ONE VERY COLD NIGHT AT THE BEGINNING of December, when the bitter wind seemed to go through the many clothes I was wearing, I watched the sow and boar emerge at 6.10 to sit above the set playfully petting one another, and grooming their coats. But the badgers seemed hesitant, alternating these short intervals of grooming and occasional stretching on the trunk of the playing tree, with furtive returns to the set for no apparent reason. The cubs appeared at several different entrances in turn, yet all seemed reluctant to leave the set. But there was a general emergence at 8 o'clock, when play and collection of bedding was suddenly in full swing, and I found my watch worth while in spite of the cold.

In my efforts to record the happenings during the winter months, I often waited in vain in high winds and nights of severe frost; conditions in which one cannot hope to see much activity. Hazards are increased for anyone approaching over frost-hardened ground, for it is impossible to walk without noise. I met a hazard of another kind on one of these frosty nights when walking across a ploughed field to reach some sets in an isolated spinney. The ground was frozen hard, and the night very dark, with promise of snow. I stumbled along over the deeply furrowed field making so much noise underfoot I feared that any badgers near the set entrance would hear my coming. I stopped to listen as I neared the spinney surrounding the sets. To my dismay, I heard the crunch of heavy boots coming towards me over the frosted field. The footsteps came gradually nearer. I peered into the darkness, but could see nothing, then, as it seemed that the walker was almost upon me, a dim shape passed a few yards distant. The sounds died away and I saw the figure of a man silhouetted against the sky as he reached higher ground.

Back in the season of late and erratic emergence, during which the weather was so cold that it became physically impossible to stand still for any length of time, I had reverted to my practice of other winters by taking up my stand a short time before I expected badgers to emerge. One night the badgers in the piggery forestalled me by emerging early. I arrived with another watcher, in time to see them at a distance, from the field outside. We waited till they seemed to have dispersed to their feeding grounds, then slowly, and quietly as possible, approached the sets, for we had come a long way and we still hoped that something of interest might occur. It was vital to get to the sets without noise, lest any badgers had remained. First we had to negotiate a barbed-wire fence, and the wire was fixed with only about twelve inches between the strands, the last of which was secured at ground level. We were obliged to roll through, and some of the clay still clings to our hard-worn garments, for the ground was wet and slippery. But we were rewarded by a sight of the boar, for he had not left the set, and other badgers returned during our watch, which terminated only when we could bear the cold no longer.

The snow of early January did not remain long. The thaw left the ground very wet, and there was great activity among the badgers. They had brought into use an old path that ran along the steep bank above the foxes' dell. At one place a smooth area round a hawthorn bush defined their playground. It was a nightly habit to clean their claws on a thick and very old clematis vine that hung in loops from the trees above. This became more and more ragged as the outer layers of bark were loosened, and hung down in long streamers from the vine. The badgers had made new dung-pits on top of the bank under the hawthorn bushes, and the open grass was the scene of much activity. Cropped areas showed where it had been taken for food and bedding, and small routing holes were evidence of the badgers' search for grubs and mice.

Since the shortage of rabbits through the myxomatosis outbreak, grass and other herbage have figured largely in the badgers' omnivorous diet. These have been eaten in quantity with grubs, earthworms, mice, voles, and other available rodents. Chance items such as wounded birds, left on the ground after a pigeon shoot, have been taken as a welcome addition to the animals' diet in hard weather. Caterpillars are always a prized delicacy. At one time I watched a colony of badgers which were continually being gassed and reduced in numbers by a prejudiced farmer, though they did no harm, and, among other useful work that passed unnoticed, cleared quantitites of caterpillars from his Brussels sprout crop. During the hard weather of January, a heap of bean and wheat chaff was thrown out in the wood near the piggery. It was sprouting and smelled horribly, but the badgers fed on it as long as it lasted, though the nourishment they derived must have been small.

Severe frosts were followed by snow. The badgers came out, and tracks indicated considerable wandering, but there was evidence that little food was gleaned. When the thaw came at the end of February, quantities of bedding were taken into set A, suggesting that cubs were in this set. On March 7 the sow again brought bedding in, and the following night a small incident confirmed my suspicions.

Several badgers had emerged from the main opening of set B, and two of last year's cubs had come across to the subsidence where they joined the sow which had brought bedding to the set the previous night. She stood above the set entrance calling softly to her cubs. The other badgers stood beside her; all listened, heads lowered to the entrance. I could hear nothing, but doubtless the whimpering of the tiny cubs was heard by the badgers. One of last year's cubs, curious to know the cause of the strange noises below, attempted to go into the set. The sow snapped angrily and pushed her aside, then went down herself, followed respectfully by the other two.

The sow was reluctant to leave the set. She came out, and finding a bundle of bedding which she had left near the set the night before, took it up in her mouth and walked towards the entrance. This was an unconventional method of carrying bedding which I had not seen before, but instinct ruled and she turned round to bring the bundle in backwards in the usual manner. Later she came out and joined the company on the grass where there was a general romp before the badgers dispersed.

I waited, hoping that the sow would return to her cubs, but there was no activity except the wanderings of a hare which came through the piggery and sat listening beside me; in search of his love, perhaps, in a peaceful setting under the stars. After a while, he ambled away, oblivious of human presence. Next morning, tell-tale traces along the path told me that bedding had been taken into the set again, and to set B. I regretted that the cold of the previous night had sent me home shivering before these activities occurred.

The renewal of bedding in set B might indicate cubs there also, and later, much chalk and old bedding was turned out of this set. The pigs had been moved to other quarters at the end of last year, which made watching more peaceful and provided a greater variety of positions from which the sets could be watched. From now, I was anxious to keep a very close watch in the hope of seeing the cubs make their first venture above ground.

In spite of careful watching, I did not find cub tracks till May 5. They were outside the second opening of set B. This fired my enthusiasm, yet I saw only one adult badger that night. But the next evening, the first badger came out from set A at 9.30, and four others followed from the main opening of this set. Then two small cubs appeared at the set entrance, and almost immediately began to play with the now full-grown cubs of last year. Meanwhile three smaller cubs of another family emerged from the second hole of set B. They were quickly joined by the other two, and all were engaged for a time digging above the set entrance. They scratched diligently, snuffing in the chalk, and nibbling scraps they picked up. It was an achievement when one managed to unearth a piece large enough to be used as a plaything.

I estimated the three younger cubs to be about seven weeks old. They were still wobbly on their legs, and delightfully fluffy, but not much inclined to play. They made short excursions round the set, and stretched full length up the hawthorn bushes, scraping the bark with their claws. The adults went away quickly, and this enabled me to get very close to the cubs, as they were almost indifferent to my presence. The older cubs, which were probably two weeks in advance of the little ones, were very boisterous in their play, and rushed helter-skelter round the sets, running, jumping, and leaping over one another, or tussling together, a jumbled ball of fur.

When a badger cub incites another to play, he fluffs his fur out at right angles to his body, making himself appear much bigger than his normal size. He then stands on stiff legs, and bounces off the ground, to come down and make a rapid dart at his opponent. He dodges back and bounces again, sometimes straight up in the air, sometimes to one side. Often, when in mid-air, he will execute a curious little twist of his body, and his nose is brought round rapidly to his tail, and back. After several advances of this kind, the other cub usually responds, and the two are off in a game, the object of which seems to be to pin one's opponent down by the throat, and keep him there. But even another badger cannot hold a kicking, biting cub down for more than a few seconds, and they are off again in another wild scramble.

The greatest advantage in this game is to achieve a good strategic position, whether by rushing up behind and seizing the other's tail, or leaping on him from above. The rules of the game allow, it seems, any method of attack providing blood is not drawn, and a cry of pain among the cubs is rarely heard. Very rough play is warned off with a puppy snarl, which usually stops the game, but only to draw breath, for the nature of the play is always good-tempered.

CUBS

WITH CUBS ABOVE GROUND IN THE PIGGERY, there were few uneventful watches. Besides the families of this season, two cubs of last year had remained. It is usual for some of the cubs to leave in their first autumn, and these are generally the boar cubs. The colony now comprised eleven badgers, and there was plenty of activity.

Often the adults went away foraging as soon as they emerged, and this gave the watcher more freedom with the cubs. For my amusement and theirs, I sometimes brought bread and syrup to the sets. At first I put some on the lower half of a post near the entrance where the cubs were likely to emerge. They soon discovered this, and gathered round to lick the syrup, and nibble the sweetened surface of the wood in their efforts to get the last drop. I also threw down other food before they emerged.

When a badger cub finds something new, he handles it with caution. One night I watched a cub which had found his first sample of bread and syrup. He sniffed it from a safe distance, then advanced and poked it gingerly with his nose. He jumped back, and regarded it for some seconds, then advanced again to nose it. This happened several times, then he dared to pat the bread with his paw. Gaining courage he seized it in his mouth, but dropped it immediately. He stood watching, as though he expected it to move, then suddenly picked it up again, and scuttled down the set with a roar of triumph!

To avoid going close to the sets near the time of emergence, I was obliged to toss the bread and syrup onto the ground outside the set entrance where I hoped the cubs would emerge. One evening I made an error of judgment which might have cost me the night's watching. There is no more difficult object to throw than a piece of bread sticky with treacle. It adheres firmly to the fingers, with the result that it fails to take off when expected, and is very difficult to direct. To my dismay, a piece fell down the set entrance. Any adult badger that chanced to use the entrance would, presumably, turn back on finding this strange object in the set. Whether a cub came there first and ate the bread, I do not know, but, to my surprise, the sow, which was the first to come from this entrance, emerged without hesitation. She was followed by three more adults, and the cubs, which remained behind to play and enjoy the syrup, licking it from the post and the tree's roots near my feet.

I had, on previous occasions, fed badgers at another set from a wooden bowl of syrup held in my hand, and I soon found that the cubs in the piggery could be tempted in the same way.

On the evening of May 25 I began my watch standing by a hawthorn near the set entrance most frequently used by the cubs. I had a bowl of syrup on the ground beside me, and it was my plan to watch the adults leave the set, then to move to the post where I had been habitually putting the syrup, and sit down hoping to feed the cubs by hand.

Two adults left and before I could move, a cub came out and went to the syrup post. It licked the treacle for some time, stretching its length up the post to reach the highest drop. A badger's nose is very adaptable, and when any surface needs to be nibbled or licked closely, can be turned up in such a wrinkled and comical fashion that it appears to be made of rubber: an attribute well demonstrated on the syrup post. When all had been gleaned from this, the cub busied himself digging a hole at the base to get the syrup that had trickled down, then finding the stick I had used as a ladle, carried his prize away down the set.

This, I thought, was my opportunity to move over to the post, where I hoped the other cubs would eventually come. But as I bent to pick up the bowl of syrup, a cub came out from the set entrance, and I could only lower myself gently where I was, and sit against the hawthorn, in the hope that the cub might come to me. After examining the treacle post and finding that someone else had been there first, it came towards me. It peeped round the base of the tree, and sniffed the syrup I held out. But in spite of its youthful trust, it was suspicious, and retired a few paces to think the matter over. There was some brushwood behind the tree, and out of the corner of my eye, I watched the cub creep cautiously round it and approach from the other side. But the syrup was not there, and I dared not move for fear of frightening the cub. It retreated again, and I could hear it rustling through the brushwood to come round and try once more from the right. It sniffed cautiously, first at the wooden bowl, then at my fingers, and started to lap the syrup. Meanwhile the other cubs had come out and were wandering round the bush. Presently, one after another came to take the syrup. While one cub was feeding, I lifted a finger to rub its chin, but the liberty was regarded with concern, and the cub withdrew from the syrup bowl, and stared at my finger. I did not move it again, and the cub returned to the feast.

Movement is one of the chief alarm factors for the badger. When the wind direction is right, and the watcher keeps still, he is usually overlooked, even in daylight if his shape is mingled with foliage or the boughs of a tree. But the slightest movement alerts the badger at once; this was obvious in the cub. The sugar stick my finger represented was in no way alarming if it remained inanimate, but its movement caused an immediate reaction.

May is a pleasant month for the watcher. The cubs are still delightfully young and playful. On the night I am reporting, the five cubs were in high spirits. After they had fed from the syrup, they remained in the area, chasing, and bouncing at, one another, often very close to my hawthorn. I was apprehensive lest the sow should discover me, for she had emerged meanwhile from the opening a few yards away. But she was clearing the set with great vigour. She brought out quantities of chalk, dragging it back with her forepaws into a heap through which her path made a channel of the kind often seen outside badgers' sets.

I had no cover except the small trunk of the hawthorn and a little brushwood behind it, but the cubs approached from all directions, often coming to within a foot of where I sat, and they showed no concern. They were out for over an hour, then retired into the set. This appears to be the usual habit of young cubs after play.

In less than a week they had gained confidence, and were making little journeys away from the sets, often returning with coats soaking wet from the dew off the fields. When wet, a badger will shake its coat like a dog, and is often invited to vigorous play, which is nature's way of warming and drying the wet animal.

By June 10 the cubs had taken up temporary residence in a set, long disused, in the bluebell wood a short distance from the piggery. Both families had returned to the piggery by June 15, and eleven badgers were again seen leaving the sets.

Such a large population made watching very entertaining, particularly when most of the badgers came out together and played in company above the sets. How they were accommodated in the set one can only imagine. They often came all from one entrance as though using the same set, but, as I have mentioned earlier, the two were probably connected underground, and it may be that both sets were in use at the time.

Sometimes the badgers went away at once to their feeding grounds, accompanied by the cubs, and on those nights watching was disappointing. There was still practically no ground cover in spite of the absence of the pigs, otherwise the badgers might sometimes have remained foraging in the area. I saw little life there apart from the hares, and a few wood-mice, the young of which had not yet learned to fear, and sometimes entertained me before the badgers came out. One night a hunting stoat came past, and it was interesting to see its scent traced by a sow badger over the entire track it had taken, long after it had gone.

During the first week in July the badgers started coming out just after 8 p.m. I had some splendid daylight watching, for they were very playful and often seemed in no hurry to go away. With five cubs in the colony, emergence was a lively and often boisterous introduction to the night's activities. But in the middle of August the population was reduced to five. Only the boar, sow, and the three youngest cubs remained, the other pair with two cubs, and two of last year's cubs had evidently gone to sets farther afield, for I could find no evidence of occupation at any of the sets in the vicinity. This change of residence may have been disastrous to them. I had reports of many gassings on adjacent farms.

The remaining family was much attracted to the bluebell wood, where they had opened a new entrance to a set that had not been in use for a long time. There were signs of great activity round it, but I never saw badgers using the set, though they came there from the piggery, and frequently took the path through the wood after emergence. I was sometimes able to hurry along the farm road to see them cross it, and go down the fence towards the banks containing the sets they used last summer. They did this in full daylight, though they had to cross the road and travel for about two hundred yards in the open field. They looked furtively round them before leaving the cover of the herbage on the edge of the wood, and one evening a badger came out before I had time to stand back against the hedge. I was completely exposed, but by good fortune I was not seen, though I was only a few yards away. The badger scurried across to the field, giving me a splendid view.

Another time, I followed to the steep bank. I could hear a badger foraging under the elders. Presently it came out onto the pasture a short distance away. It stared in my direction, then turned away, snuffing in the grass. It visited the hole used earlier by the foxes, and after a leisured wandering in the pasture, went down the bank to disappear under the elder bushes, and I was left in lonely contemplation, envying its happy state as I stood looking after it in the starlit night.

LIFE BEGINS

EVERY NATURALIST HOPES TO WITNESS something new in animal behaviour, but such revelations are rare. A long time may elapse without the reward of any dramatic discovery. But meanwhile the study of wild life is never without compensation in those experiences of intimacy and beauty which come to us all from time to time in the field. The unaccountable moment when some wild animal puts its trust in us, or the long awaited coming above ground of young cubs; the finding of a tiny leveret in the grass; the glimpse of a fawn lying in dappled sunlight; these and many other chance encounters help to make our efforts worth while.

Perhaps no more delightful incident can be witnessed than the first venture of cubs above ground. All young creatures have great charm, and the choice of species makes little difference to the fascination of the scene when young cubs view the world for the first time in the twilight of a spring evening. The badger cub looks very small as he sits down outside the set to survey the strange scene before him, but he appears unconcerned by this first visit above ground, and the new surroundings are accepted with sleepy-eyed indifference. The waking realization of light and form in a scene vastly different from the one the cub has known underground arouses no apprehension. Nature has equipped him for this moment, and he accepts the change with philosophical indifference.

The cub soon begins to explore his surroundings. He tries his teeth on any small piece of wood found near the set entrance, and crawling insects awake a keen sense of curiosity. He discovers strange scents snuffed under the surface, and digs for them with sharp, little claws. Or he may sit for a while listening to the night sounds; a small, fluffy form taking his share of joy from life, content with the moment, neither able nor wishing to know what the future may bring. The scene as yet holds no fears for him. Even the form of the watcher is accepted, for there are many similar shapes: trees, bushes, tangles of weed and briar; one shape more or less makes no difference, unless it should move suddenly or make an unaccustomed sound.

Six weeks is the earliest age at which cubs are likely to be seen above ground. Before this they remain in the underground chamber which the sow keeps warmly lined with clean, dry bedding. The sustenance she provides and her comforting presence are their entire world.

It would be heartless to attempt to dig out a badger's breeding den, and no naturalist would support such action, though his longing to see the cubs might be very great. But last February this privilege came to some members of a local hunt when they inadvertently disclosed a den containing a litter of young cubs.

A fox was thought to have gone to earth in an artificial drain laid as a trap. It was constructed with two tunnels leading to a box which formed an underground chamber about two feet by four, over which a wooden, turf-covered lid had been placed for the purpose of inspection. When the lid was removed the box was found to contain four young badger cubs lying together in a "nest" of bracken. Their eyes were not yet open, and they were therefore less than ten days old. Fortunately the cover was replaced without delay. A week later the underground chamber was opened again by the hunt as only a few of their number had been present on the previous occasion, and others now hoped to see the cubs. They found the den empty, for the sow had moved her cubs to another set. Badgers are extremely timid, but with the usual courage of animals when their young are in danger, she had returned, and moved each cub a distance of from five to six hundred yards, assuming that she took them to the nearest set. I would have given much to have watched her that night, but I heard of the incident too late, though I was able to examine the empty breeding chamber and to make sketches of it. The box was thickly lined with bracken which had been broken down into short lengths making a soft, close, bedding material, which was doubtless very warm. Whether the bracken had been crushed into this state incidentally when gathered and brought to the den, or whether it had been purposely trampled by the sow I cannot say. Another noteworthy feature was the extreme cleanliness of the bedding, for it showed no sign of having been in use. The badger's attention to hygiene is a well-known characteristic, and cubs are never allowed to lie on soiled bedding.

It is delightful to see a sow badger emerging with very young cubs, one of which may be seen coming to the set entrance to peep out between the protective cover of her front legs. These occasions rarely pass without some attention to grooming which has a suggestion of fondling on the sow's part. She keeps the cubs in spotless condition. They are small replicas of the parents though their coats are lighter in colour and there is a general fluffiness in their appearance which adds much to their charm. When they first emerge from the set their legs have not yet gained their full strength, and the badger cubs' progression is somewhat uncertain. A large piece of chalk or stone under the paws, or the rough approach of a playful companion may send a cub rolling, but it matters little to a badger cub which way up he is, and rolling on his back is something he will indulge in with apparent pleasure from time to time even through adult life.

There is little play among the cubs in their first few appearances, but they soon gain strength and then play is a nightly occurrence. Their first interest is in pieces of wood and chalk, or stones which they find near the set openings. They are nosed with interest; picked up and nibbled, and sometimes carried into the set. They are treasured possessions, and the smallest cub will snarl fiercely if he meets another who may attempt to take his prize on the way down.

By the time the cubs are steady on their legs they have become more active generally. They have learned to clean their claws by scraping them down the bark of trees or bushes near the set, and play becomes frequent among the cubs and parents, though vigorous bouts at this age are usually followed by a rest in the set.

At the sets I was watching most during 1957 two litters of cubs were born, and one night I had the pleasure of seeing six fluffy little fellows emerge together. I knew that barring unforeseen disaster a successful season of watching could be expected.

During the early part of May I had some disappointing watches, for the cubs frequently failed to come above ground though I waited long after the parents had left the sets. Yet I often found next day that the cubs had been out later, for their claw marks, and sometimes a few of their hairs, were left on a board on which I had put down some honey or syrup. For a week I did not see the cubs at all, then one night two followed the adults out and there was a lot of play among all the badgers. Though there were two families of cubs there was only one boar and it was assumed that the smaller of the two sows had lost her mate.

A friend who joined me one night watched an outlying set which appeared to be in use, and his observations are of interest as they show how deceptive the apparently active set may be. Spoor had been seen at the entrance to this outlying set, and clearly marked paths connected a number of entrances, but no badgers emerged. Though soon after the three adults had left the set I was watching they were seen to come along the path to the outlying set. They ran by nose to tail, the boar leading followed by the smaller of the two

sows, with the second sow close behind her. Each badger stopped in turn and looked into the set, then went on his or her way. The remains of a dead hare, probably the victim of a fox, were lying in their path: these they sniffed but left untouched. At another set that I watched this summer I arrived one evening to find a partly eaten hare lying outside the opening. Later a badger approached the entrance from above, having come along the path from another opening to the set. He stopped suddenly when he came to the hare, and drew back, which indicated that it was not a badger's kill, and was probably left there by a fox. The badger stretched out his nose towards the dead hare and sniffed it cautiously. When he had assured himself that man had no part in placing it there, he backed into the set, and with one vigorous pull took the hare down after him. I saw no more of it except one front paw which lay across the roots of the playing tree next evening.

By the second week in May the six cubs of the other colony were following the parents on journeys of about forty yards from the sets, but they did not go away with them on their nightly rambles, and returned to go into or play near the sets. Their appearances were still erratic. One exceptionally good evening of observation, when they remained for a long time taking syrup almost at my feet, was followed by another when storms and high winds kept the cubs in the set, though next evening a return to calm weather failed to bring them out.

Though the sow badger is exceptionally wary while newly born cubs are in the set, soon after they are accustomed to coming above ground she seems to show little concern for their safety, and will often leave them almost at once after emergence. The cubs then remain outside the set alone, and as they have little fear at this age, can be observed more freely than in the presence of the adults when the watcher may alert the badgers by the slightest sound or movement.

This freedom from fear is shown by most very young animals. Litters of young rabbits can be approached within a few feet while they continue sunning themselves unconcernedly outside the burrows. The same characteristic is seen in young mice and voles. Fox cubs, too, have less fear of man when they first come above ground. The chance of their accepting the watcher's presence without undue concern is greatest at this early age. But first the naturalist must find an earth suitable to his purpose as not every litter of fox cubs is easily accessible for study. Many times I have had to abandon my hopes of seeing fox cubs lest my presence should draw unwanted attention to their whereabouts.

BADGERS' TOUCH

THROUGH THE YEARS WHILE I HAVE WATCHED badgers intensively my contacts with them have gradually become closer till the touch of a cub's nose on my hand, or his tongue exploring my fingers for the food I offer, has become a delightful and intimate part of my watching. This has enabled me to see and study the animals at much closer range than I had at first thought possible. I have found that the chief difficulty is not in gaining their confidence, but in being in the right place at the right time.

As soon as cubs are above ground in the spring I put the lure of honey or syrup on the roots of a tree or any other suitable place near the set, choosing a position where it will be possible for me to sit on the ground and feed the badgers. As soon as they have found the food and begin coming to it regularly I sit near and wait for the badgers to emerge. On finding me for the first time the cubs hesitate a little but soon take the food from my hand.

Though I have found it possible to feed adult badgers they are more difficult than the cubs as they are always very suspicious and wary. The cubs are less cautious, and there is usually one in a litter more tame than the rest. In the spring of 1957 the colony I was watching comprised a boar, his sow, another sow, which had lost her mate, and six cubs. Each of the sows had three cubs, and one litter was born about a week earlier than the other. The smallest cub in the younger litter was exceptionally tame, and after she had been taking food from my hand for a time, I was able to stroke her as she fed. Apart from her small size, she was easily distinguished from the others as the black under her jaws was suffused into the white cheeks, almost meeting the dark line over her head below the ears. She looked as though she had snuffed in a soot bag.

I was not able to feed the cubs by hand as soon as I had hoped, for weather conditions and some unknown factor had made their emergence very erratic during the early spring. At one time they disappeared from the scene entirely for a week, and I wondered if they had met disaster, but this was unlikely as they were not venturing far from the entrances, and the sets were undisturbed.

The main obstacle to feeding the badgers was the possibility of being discovered by the adults. As the cubs were not going far from the set it was necessary for me to be near the entrance to feed them, and it was very difficult to hide myself completely, for the badgers were emerging in daylight. I waited therefore a short distance away and moved to the appointed place after the adults had left the area. This could be achieved even in daylight with the cubs very close. But occasionally my plans went astray. If the cubs came out shortly before or with the parents I had to wait till the adults had gone, and this sometimes meant that the cubs would have licked all the honey off the tree, and returned into the set before I could reach the chosen place.

When they had been coming above ground for some time they began using more than one opening to the set, and this added to my difficulties as I had to find a suitable place to feed them at each.

"Cubs taking syrup from tree roots.
4.20 p.m. June 21/57".

Fortunately they emerged most frequently from the one they had first used, and this was well situated, with a hawthorn against which I could sit on the ground undetected about eight feet from the set entrance. Here I was successful even when the adults emerged in full light.

When I missed feeding the cubs I was able to watch and sketch them at close range. It was invaluable to see them in detail during daylight, and they often remained a long time licking the tree's roots persistently, pushing their noses up into wrinkles against the bark in their efforts to extract the last drop of sweetness. When the honey ran down the tree and off the roots to the ground, the cubs busied themselves digging for it. I also put some on a hollow piece of board, and this was scraped, nibbled, and pushed along with great vigour, in the hope that it would yield more. Sometimes when the feast was over the cubs retired to the set entrance where they sat cleaning their sticky paws, a task in which they assisted one another with relish.

In June the badger colony moved to an adjacent bluebell wood, and I had to find a new place where the cubs might be persuaded to feed. The set was a small one with only three entrances which made my task easier, but suitable feeding places were scarce. A half-rotten stub looked a likely situation with entrances to left and right about five feet away. This proved to be a useful watching position when the wind was favourable. A good view could be obtained by standing up on the stub, and to feed the cubs I crawled in under the overhanging end, sheltered by this, and a small elder bush on the other side. The only disadvantage of the position was the narrow space in which I had to sit or kneel. I was very cramped and made horribly uncomfortable by a piece of the stub which jutted out and could not be avoided in any position. I tried to make some improvement by daylight but I could not remove the offending piece without using a saw. This entailed too much risk of disturbance, for I knew, from the directions of the entrances, that the set must be underneath the stub. It was also a very shallow set where doubtless many sounds from above could be heard. Some of the elder twigs which I pushed into the ground to give cover seemed to go through into space after the first few inches of soil. This may have been only where the roots of the dead tree had rotted away, but I often wondered if I should suddenly descend into the badgers' sleeping quarters.

One morning when clearing a path to the set to ensure a quiet approach by night, I stopped to look down the main entrance, and to my surprise saw a cub walking past inside. The opening had been excavated into the side of an existing underground chamber, and the cub was making his way across it. He did not see me but I wondered if my activities, though conducted quietly, had disturbed him. I believe that badgers are more often awake by day than we suppose. I have seen both cubs and adults abroad at mid-morning, and farm workers have told me of incidents when badgers have been seen at this time. Possibly such animals were making a late return to the set having remained hidden above ground till an unusually late hour. I presume that most of this behaviour occurs in summer when there is plenty of cover, though I was regularly told of an instance when a badger was seen crossing a ploughed field one mid-morning in early spring.

The night of June 15 was warm and fine; the badgers in the bluebell wood emerged at 9.25. A cub appeared first, looking wistfully from the opening under the elder roots. Presently he came out to explore further, and wandered along the path, where he encountered a beetle making its nightly round. The cub quickly became engrossed, hurrying the beetle on its way with not very gentle snuffles and snorts. Meanwhile one of the sows had emerged. She strolled along the path unnoticed by the cub, and startled him. He about-turned with lightning speed, and let out an angry snarl. The sow went on a few steps then stopped and looked back over her shoulder accusingly, as a parent might look at a rude child. But after a few moments she trotted away, her grey skirts bobbing; a benign figure, her motherly heart full of forgiveness. Such is the charm of the summer night!

After the adults had gone the cubs remained foraging in the area near the set, and it was not long before our sheltering tree-stub became involved in their wanderings. I was kneeling in my usual

cramped position by the stub, and my companions had climbed up on top. But we had overlooked a torch left lying on the ground behind us. A cub discovered this, smelt it, doubted its credentials, and fled. This sent the other cubs scuttling back to the set, and all went in. But an enquiring little face soon appeared at another opening, and one of the cubs ventured out again. He wandered down the slope to the edge of the wood, where he began to scrape industriously in the soil. After a few minutes he came back carrying in his mouth what appeared to be a long-dead rat. He put his burden down near the set and began nosing it, intent on enjoying the unexpected delicacy. Suddenly a roosting pigeon flapped its wings overhead. The cub raced for the set. But as he reached the entrance he regained his self-possession, remembering that he had heard these sounds before, and they could be ignored with safety. He looked back at his capture, and returned to claim it. He carried it to the nearest badger path, and with much tearing and scrunching ate every scrap. To my disappointment no mite of fur or bone was left to prove the victim's identity.

After a while the other cubs emerged. I had put down a tin of honey at arm's length. The smallest cub soon found it, and started to lap the honey with sounds of relish which increased in volume every time a raisin was discovered. The badger eats noisily, expressing a full appreciation, for he has the gourmet's relish of good food. But his choice is wider than ours: equal enjoyment is derived from a dish of raisins and honey, or a succulent meal of very old rat.

The cub was determined to leave nothing in the tin. She licked and licked persistently in an attempt to get the raisins lodged round the lower rim. She then began to drag the tin along with her paw, biting savagely at pieces of fallen wood and other debris which hampered her progress from time to time along the path. In this way she proceeded towards the set entrance, stopping occasionally for another lick round the tin. Finally she picked it up and carried it to the set, but with some hesitation, for it had a tendency to swing, and clatter against her legs. She struggled to hold it but the tin was very slippery, and it was unlike any prey she had captured before. She approached the set from above the entrance, and stood hesitating. She was faced with a drop down, which was awkward with such a troublesome burden. After contemplating the problem, she dropped the tin, and went into the set without it. But she soon returned, and with front paws resting on the tree roots above the opening, studied her problem again. No inspiration was forthcoming, and she wandered away. I hoped to recover the tin before I left, as it was a useful one for the purpose, and unlike most tins was not sharp on the edge. But the cub was not going to give in easily. She came back; sniffed it and picked it up again. She stood on the roots above the set with the tin in her mouth, considering once more how she might get it down to the set. The simple solution of walking round to the front of the entrance did not occur to her. As she stood contemplating, the tin began to slide. It was a reluctant victim; the badger's instinctive method of subduing her prey then came into action. Normally it would have been shaken vigorously but the difficulty of keeping a firm hold on the tin's slippery surface did not permit these tactics. She swung it slowly from side to side, but it did not react as intended, and became even more awkward to handle. Finally she made up her mind to jump down. She dropped the tin with a clatter as she went. It rolled into the set entrance, and the cub tumbled after it. For some time she could be heard licking out the remaining honey, and pushing the tin ahead of her down the set. The sounds became fainter and fainter as she went farther underground, and eventually ceased.

The following night I again squeezed in between the tree stub and the elder bush with a supply of honey, nuts and raisins, and waited for the badgers to emerge. The smallest cub quickly came to the place where the honey had been found the night before. I held out a dish and she soon discovered it. When she had started to lap the contents I put the dish down and offered her some honey from my hand. She took it at once, nibbling my fingers and pushing her nose and muzzle down into my hand, till she had licked it clean.

When I turned it over she obligingly washed the back too.

The badgers were now using two sets in the wood. I had heard them coming out from a set across the dell, the lower end of which bordered the area containing the set I was watching. I went to the wood next morning and found the second set under the roots of a big oak tree on top of the dell. It was an easy one to watch as the bole of the oak gave good cover and beside the tree a small elder bush made another good watching position. The roots of the oak were entwined about the stump of another tree, long since fallen. This jumble of great roots was worn smooth by generations of badgers at play and there were signs of much activity round the set. One path led to a small clearing in the wood where the grass had been torn up and taken by the badgers for bedding. Several paths were in use and led to a maze of others in the wood. The scene held so much promise that although I had the company of my sister, and we could have watched both sets, we decided to remain together that night watching this one only. But in the perverse way of badgers the entire colony emerged from the other set that night.

We have developed the craft of moving about by night, and we made our way out of the wood and walked round the edge to reach a path leading to the other set. Fortunately I had kept this clear, and we made a silent approach. At 9.20 the boar and sow emerged and went away. The cubs were already out, wandering somewhere in the wood, and at 9.55 several returned to the set. The smallest cub came in search of honey, which owing to my late arrival I had not put out. But I managed to get down beside the stub while the cub was a short distance away, and after a while she came back and took syrup, raisins and peanuts from my hand. Meanwhile I stroked her face and a sticky paw with which she held the syrup dish. She remained feeding for twenty minutes then wandered away. The other cubs entertained us close to the set till midnight when, after a silence which assured us that all had left the area, we went home.

After further watching of the set below the dell we divided to observe both sets in the wood. For two nights we saw only the adult badgers and wondered whether the cubs had gone to an outlying set, but on the night of June's longest day when we watched the set below the oak, the sow, boar, and five cubs emerged together in full daylight. They all sat on the platform outside the set grooming and playing, and later foraged near-by or chased one another through the bushes, rarely going out of sight. They were completely oblivious of the watchers standing barely eight feet above the set.

After a time the sow went away through the grass clearing, and

later the boar wandered out of the wood to the lucerne field. Two of the cubs followed him but came back to join the others near the set. At about 9.30 two came up to the bole of the oak tree and began to lick the honey I had spread on the roots. The sooty-faced cub came at once to my hand, and I ladled out the sticky mixture of honey and raisins on my fingers. She remained taking it from my hand for a long time, while I stroked her cheeks and muzzle. Meanwhile the second cub was endeavouring to extract the last drops of honey from the rough bark of the tree. When he could find no more he came up behind the small cub, and gave her a sudden push, as a hint to get out of the way and let him come to my hand. She showed her resentment by snapping at the nearest thing, which chanced to be my fingers!

Though she was the smallest of the litter she would not be bullied, and a second push from behind brought her round quickly on the intruder. There was a scuffle and the second cub retired leaving Sooty-face to the feast. She was completely engrossed as she licked the honey from my hand; chewing each nut and raisin, as it was found, with noisy disregard of manners. Even my fondling was borne with indifference if such delights were given in exchange. After twenty minutes, during which she fed without pause, she trotted away through the wood. When she had gone, two more cubs came to the honey, but they were not so trusting. I waited, still on my knees, and presently another cub came to feed, nibbling my fingers and licking my hand repeatedly as he took the honey.

After the badgers left the sets in the bluebell wood they occupied several different sets in succession. These proved unsuitable situations for feeding the animals, and it was not till they returned to the sets which were to be their winter quarters, that I was able to feed them again.

The cubs were now almost equal in size to the adults. It was doubtful whether they could be persuaded to take food from my hand, for at this age they had become more wary. They were unlikely to display the trust they had shown when feeding from my hand earlier, but I felt it was worth trying. I put down some bread and syrup near the place where I hoped to feed them, but they sniffed it and turned away. I had previously had this experience when feeding cubs late in the season, and it may be that they lose some of their taste for sweet things as they grow older. If I was to have any success temptation must take another form. The next night I raided the larder, and took with me a supply of Cheddar cheese, pieces of which I threw onto the ground near the set. A boar cub was the first to find the cheese. He sniffed it, but he was suspicious, and drew back several times before taking a piece. He carried it gently in his mouth as though afraid of crushing it, and trotted away a short distance to put it down with the same care. The cheese must have smelled strongly of my hand for I had thrown it down only half an hour before. He sniffed it again, then dispensing with all scruples, quickly devoured it, picking up every crumb he had dropped. He came back, nose down sniffing the ground till he discovered another piece. This was eaten at once, and he began a search for more. When he had found and eaten several pieces he wandered off to join the other cubs at play. But later he returned and took some more cheese which I had scattered near the bush where I hoped to feed him the next evening.

I had no opportunity to prepare a place for watching, by daylight, but I arrived early the following evening and carefully removed some of the most vicious, thorny twigs that littered the

ground under the bush where I intended to sit. The cover was slight, and I picked a piece of seeding fennel, and leant it against the bush to help to break up my outline. I was almost surrounded by set openings: one in front within six feet of the bush; another eight feet away to the left; a third a little further off to my right, and the main entrance straight ahead at a distance of about twenty feet. The hawthorn bush was bare of foliage to a height of several feet above the ground, and I had a good view of all the openings. But the badgers had an equally clear view of me.

As on the previous evening the boar emerged first from the main entrance followed by two cubs. All stayed grooming for a while then went away to their feeding grounds. My hopes of a profitable evening began to fade. But a third cub soon came out to wander among the bushes. He remembered last night's cheese, and trotted boldly towards my hawthorn. I had thrown out a few crumbs to lure him in the right direction, and he quickly discovered these. But to my disappointment, having eaten them, he wandered to the set opening on my left where he had found some cheese the night before. He was unlucky, for I had avoided putting any where it might entice him away from me. There was an almost unimpeded view from the set entrance to my hawthorn, and when the cub stopped searching for cheese he lifted his head, and stared in my direction, scenting the air. He came slowly forward till he was within a few inches of my feet. He snuffed my shoes, and drew back. All hope of feeding him tonight now appeared to be gone, but he walked past my legs, apparently undeterred and came to the bole of the hawthorn to stretch his head out towards my hand holding the cheese. His nose touched my fingers, and he backed away, but after a little hesitation the delectable scent of English Cheddar overcame caution, and a cold nose was thrust into my hand. This time the cub trotted away with a generous piece of cheese. He retired beyond the bushes to eat it, carefully retrieving every crumb before returning for more.

Meanwhile I had broken the remaining cheese into small pieces to detain him longer. At first he had difficulty in distinguishing between my hand and the food, and tried to seize my fingers. But they were not to his taste, and he soon discovered that by nosing further into my hand more cheese could be found. He had many helpings before he was satisfied, and cheese became a very successful lure.

There is an indefinable charm in the touch of a wild animal's muzzle on one's hand. As I rose from my cramped position I felt I had again been fully rewarded.

GROWING UP

WHEN BADGER CUBS REACH THE STAGE OF regularly following the parents away from the sets on their nightly rambles watching is not so easy. For the animals go away to their feeding grounds and the sets are likely to remain deserted for many hours. At this season another difficulty arises, for it is a restless time of year and the badgers frequently change their sets. After June the colony I was watching moved house and I had some trouble to find them. I put in a lot of time inspecting all the sets on the farm, and watching at night but the results were poor and not infrequently I failed to see the badgers at all. At one time I lost sight of them entirely for a while when they were using a set beyond standing crops which I could not cross without risk of damage.

I found them eventually in a set excavated in a shallow bank beyond some cornfields, but though I was able to reach it by walking along the edge of a pasture, the badgers had so much cover in the undergrowth that watching there was not very successful. After a while they left this set and I lost them again, but by the end of July they were back in the main set, which they had used in the past winter and spring. Here there was practically no ground cover, and watching was up to its old standards. The night of July 20 was very lively. The entire colony including the smaller sow, which I had not seen for a time, were in residence. The boar and the bigger sow were inseparable, running everywhere together, and there was an attempted mating between them.

The many entrances to the two sets which were connected underground were mostly in use, with badgers appearing at each in turn. When they came above ground they raced away to come back in a few minutes and go down into the sets again, reappearing and coming back out shortly after. They seemed like a family returned to an old and much-loved house after a holiday, exploring every room to see if all was the same as they left it.

The cubs, now about five months old, fluffed out their coats and bounced at one another as in their earlier play. One turned on the smallest, bouncing at her with the characteristic little twist of the body in mid-air, and the two tussled and romped together, till tiring of play they trotted off towards the bluebell wood.

The badger had cubs only once a year though there are two mating periods. The second of these is from July to September, and as a result excitement often reaches a peak during these months. The cubs do not become sexually mature till the following spring but their enthusiasm for play is no less. One night soon after the badgers returned to the winter set there was another bout of great activity.

I arrived later than usual and was nearly caught in the act by a sow who emerged at 7.55. A lot of "talking" could be heard from badgers inside the sets where there were also sounds of play underground. As on the night of July 20 the badgers went in and out of the sets frequently before full emergence. A short time was spent in grooming then a sow seized the tail of the nearest cub and shook him by it. This sent them all off in a wild gambol. The sows raced away followed by the boar. But they soon came running back and scrambled down the set, then away again with the boar hard on their heels. The six cubs were also out playing. One met the returning boar who pounced on him in play, and a chase began. The badgers raced round and round the hawthorn bushes, and back over the set; off again, pounding the earth as they circled and chased, and grappled together, scampering away at last to disappear from view in the undergrowth. But the boar and three cubs soon returned and there was more play among them. They were in high spirits, which subsided little even when one found himself alone. The irrepressible spirit of fun still kept him bouncing and running circles for his own amusement.

The situation was promising but in nature nothing can be anticipated. Some very good watching followed but the badgers were now not so active. The harvesting of surrounding fields accounted in some measure for this, and there was probably a slowing down of sexual excitement. I thought the badgers had decided to remain in this set, but I was mistaken. Apparently dissatisfied with all eight sets on the farm, they excavated a new one early in August.

The set was found one night shortly before the time of emergence. It was pleasantly situated on the edge of an area overgrown with thyme and other wild flowers, but it was difficult to reach and my sister, who had discovered it, generously made her thorn-tangled way back to fetch me from the main set where my watch would have been fruitless. It was impossible to approach the new set without making some noise, and we were obliged to crawl almost on hands and knees under tangles of wild-rose and hawthorn bushes. Yet miraculously the badgers emerged.

At 8.40 the boar arrived, having come from another set. He went down the entrance, and came out again after an interval. This time he scented our footsteps, but was not much disturbed, and after taking a long sniff at the place where we had walked, retired slowly into the set again. At 9.5 he came out and indulged in a satisfying scratch in which we should have been glad to join, for the midges were tormenting us beyond endurance. A sow and one cub were the next to emerge, and it was obvious that the boar, who had spent the day away from the family, had called to fetch them. The entire colony of three adults and six cubs were seen. They wandered in and out of the set, threading their way through the thyme-scented clearing, a setting which under the harvest moon made the scene one of the most pleasant I have witnessed in years of badger watching.

The badgers were in no hurry to leave, and came back to the set entrance many times, sitting down to groom their coats, or to listen idly to the night sounds. Some of the cubs were very near to discovering us when they ran almost to the foot of some small bushes which were our only cover. But fortunately they all remained to windward, and were completely oblivious of our company. In time they wandered away, and the last we saw of them that night was the scuttling, grey figure of one who was caught in the light of our headlamps on the farm road. The set in the thyme clearing was shallow, and the colony evidently found it crowded, for they soon returned to the main set for the coming autumn and winter.

By August the cubs are nearly as big as the parents, and it is sometimes difficult to tell them apart unless one can get a view in good light. But though the general appearance is similar there are differences: the white fur on the sides of the face is thicker in the adults, giving them a wider "ruff" below the ears. This is most obvious when the badgers are seen full-face. From the profile view the cubs still have the characteristic slimness, though the domed

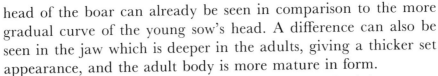

head of the boar can already be seen in comparison to the more gradual curve of the young sow's head. A difference can also be seen in the jaw which is deeper in the adults, giving a thicker set appearance, and the adult body is more mature in form.

In autumn differences in behaviour of cubs and adults are not easily distinguished. The cubs share in the task of clearing out the sets, a job which begins in earnest during September. Recently I have watched a lot of work being done on a set where one colony has moved in for the winter. The set is in chalk and sand, and at a newly opened entrance a cartload of chalk has been turned out in the past week or two. Many others have also been freshly excavated, and a lot of bedding has been brought in, though some bundles still await collection near the set.

One night I saw several badgers, including two cubs, clearing out the set together. They took turns at the work, though sometimes when the boar and the sow were both attempting to bring out loads from underground they were frequently in one another's way. The boar was pushed aside unceremoniously by the sow on several occasions as she struggled out backwards with her heavy load. He seemed eventually to become disheartened. Like some husbands whose attempts to help in the kitchen are not appreciated, he wandered away, but doubtless with a clear conscience, having done his best.

Exactly what happens to each of the badger cubs as they grow up it is not possible to tell. Certainly some leave the colony in late autumn, and these appear to be the male cubs. Others remain with the family and I usually see some cubs of the past year with the family through the following spring and summer. But the badger's life is arranged in such a way that overcrowding does not occur in the sets. Through the many years I have watched badgers I have found that the number in a colony returns to approximately the same level each winter. This is brought about by the eventual dispersal of the cubs. The badger's way of living does not tolerate overcrowding in a set, which would result in dirty conditions. No one need hesitate to give sanctuary to such a clean-living animal, or fear that the colonies will increase beyond their normal limits of population. Yet the badger is much persecuted. He does a vast amount of good and negligible harm but comparatively few farmers allow him to remain unmolested. Many believe the old misconceptions about the animals' feeding habits, but if they would avail themselves of the first-hand knowledge which naturalists have gained by scientific study of the badger, they would see in him an ally well worth encouraging on their land.

BADGERS' MOON

FOR ME BADGERS AND MOONLIGHT ARE indivisible. To look out across a moonlit countryside is immediately to picture the animals at play by the sets, or foraging along their paths. For badgers have an affinity with this scene of half-veiled light.

My diaries over the years contain many entries which, even when brief, recall the thrill of moonlit occasions. The clear atmosphere of winter when the moon travels high, gives brilliant light and dense contrasts of tone in which it is possible to hide oneself effectively. But the animals can also hide in these conditions, and the watcher is fortunate when a badger is bold enough to come out of the shadows, and cross a clearing in the full light of the moon. A perfect February night, moonlit, still, and warm for the time of year, recorded in my notes, tells how I missed seeing some of the emerging badgers as they crept away from the set in deep shadow. But sounds of "wickering" and purring in the entrance told me there were still some badgers in the set, and suddenly the boar emerged in full light, followed by the sow. The bank on which they stood among moonlit grass, became at once a place of enchantment. But the badgers, awake to the possibility of danger, lifted their heads to sniff the air expectantly, hoping to decipher the many scents and sounds which came to them from a landscape in which the normal composition of trees and bushes around the set, appeared in bewildering contrasts of light and shade. Though this was February, pigeons cooed intermittently, and sometimes a song-thrush or blackbird, disturbed by the unaccustomed brilliance of the moon, twittered anxiously, and changed its roost. Across the sky came the shrill call of a passing wader.

Moonlight may awaken a variety of birds, and those which are normally on the wing after dark, or are night songsters, are inspired to give voice more fully. Owls are often very active and conversational under the moon. Recently several tawnys held a conference near my bedroom window, trilling and wailing in the clear moonlight of the early hours. But this is a usual sound of the night, and it is the unexpected song of a small passerine, as a dunnock who sings a short stanza spontaneously from his roost, which brings the greatest enchantment.

Less brilliant than the moonlit contrasts of winter, but more comfortable for the watcher, is the warm twilight of summer evenings when the moon takes over at sundown while the birds are still singing. Then the badgers can be seen in good light, and sow and boar will often sit outside the set grooming each other's coats, whilst the cubs are at play.

These are leisured nights for most mammals, with hares browsing on the hill, and badger cubs finding new joy in their growing strength and ability to wander farther afield. But the lush herbage of summer is a disadvantage to the watcher, for it may entirely screen the animal from view, even in moonlight. Sets in bracken often become useless for observation at this time of year, when the animals can emerge and go away without showing even the tip of a snout. Paths and ditches are obscured by herbage wherein foxes, badgers, and small deer form tunnels for themselves, and travel miles without being seen. The watcher can then only guess what may lie beyond the still beauty of the meadows and harvest fields.

I would find it difficult to choose the night or month in which a moonlit watch could give most pleasure. Each is, perhaps, in its immediate moments the most desirable. But when the chill of winter has gone, and the spring's first warmth is felt in a still April evening, the sounds of the night give the watcher a great feeling of aspiration. The upsurge of joy in the birds' song is at its richest and most inspiring. On such a night when I was out from sundown onward at my favourite badgers' set, the song-thrushes dominated all other sounds. Many birds had chosen the top of the hawthorn thicket, above the sets, from which to give this outpouring of song before nightfall. The volume and brilliance of their calls were almost overwhelming, for, unaware of the listener, several birds sang only a few yards away. From a full crescendo the singing gradually diminished, till in the ensuing silence one thrush, having outsung all others, called his last triumphant notes, and was away to his roost. In the quiet dusk I could hear the mournful cry of a little owl, far off on the opposite hillside. A fox repeated his sudden short bark in the wood behind me. The confidential notes of pheasants came from the hawthorns where they shared the roost of thrushes and other small birds. A wheeling plover called, and I heard the rhythmic beat of wings as a flock of migratory birds swept over the tree-tops, and were gone.

A badger emerged slowly, and paused, listening to the seductive cooing of a pigeon in the wood. The moon's first quarter shone out from behind thin, drifting cloud, and I thought for a moment that I should be seen. The badger's attention was riveted on the hawthorn against which I was endeavouring to appear as one with the twisted branches. Overhead the moon hung, splendidly remote from this small but desirable corner of these acres. After further scrutiny the badger, deciding, perhaps, that the additional bulk of the tree was merely an illusion created by a trick of light and shadows, wandered away. One after another the badgers of the colony emerged to dally for a while above the sets before taking the path of the first to leave. Where did they go? And what did they glean on their night's wandering? Perhaps if I had followed I would have found them foraging on the near-by pasture. But they may have gone far along the hedge bottoms, or through the woods where fallen twigs and leaves underfoot would defeat any efforts to follow without being heard.

In autumn, when badgers clean out their sets for winter habitation, the moon may give the watcher good opportunities to see the animals at work. Sets in chalk form a white background against which the badgers are likely to be seen to advantage. One evening in October I watched a sow working for a long time to clear a set. Chalk had been drawn out yearly, making a huge hummock by the entrance. As she worked, the fresh chalk she excavated was lit by the moon, and I could see all her movements clearly as she came out, dragging her burden between her paws, to throw it back vigorously as she reached the end of the gully formed by her many journeys across the heap.

To see badgers above ground in snow is one of the most thrilling sights of the naturalist's winter. If to this scene can be added the splendour of moonlight and shadows across the unbroken snow, winter has paid all her debts to the long-suffering watcher.

When Eileen fell ill in March 1989, at the age of almost eighty-four, both she and her sister Eva (who was eighty-nine, and unable to look after herself) were taken into hospital, then to a nursing home. Friends who went to their house discovered, in the studio, an amazing cache of pictures by the Sopers, father and daughter, among them more than 300 watercolours of wildlife painted by Eileen. The pictures reproduced in this book were part of that hidden hoard.

For the past fifteen years Eva had been bedridden, and Eileen had been forced to devote herself to household chores, spending less and less time in her studio. Yet both had retained their keen interest in wild creatures, and great was their delight when badgers appeared in the garden, coming to feed under a light on the terrace, at a point where Eva could see them from her upstairs window.

With the old sisters temporarily out of action, the family solicitors put in hand plans to refurbish the house, so that the Sopers could come back to it, with nurses living in. Many improvements were made – new bathrooms, a stair-lift and so on – and one evening while work was in progress a painter was startled by a noise at the door. Opening it, he found a badger which had arrived for its supper.

Alas, both sisters died soon afterwards, before they could return home. But was it not extraordinarily poignant that Brock should still come in search of food, not knowing that by then his human mentor was too far gone to help him?